EARTHLINGS

SAYAKA MURATA

**Translated from the Japanese
by Ginny Tapley Takemori**

GRANTA

Granta Publications, 12 Addison Avenue, London W11 4QR

First published in Great Britain by Granta Books, 2020
This paperback edition published by Granta Books, 2021
Originally published in the United States in 2020 by Grove Press,
an imprint of Grove Atlantic, Inc., New York

A CIP catalogue record for this book is available from the British Library.

3 5 7 9 10 8 6 4 2

ISBN 978 1 78378 569 8 (paperback)
ISBN 978 1 78378 568 1 (ebook)

Originally published as *Chikyu seijin*. Japanese edition published by
SHINCHOSHA Publishing Co., Ltd., Tokyo. English language translation
rights reserved to Grove Atlantic, Inc. under license granted by
Sayaka Murata arranged with SHINCHOSHA Publishing Co., Ltd.
through The English Agency (Japan) Ltd.

JAPANFOUNDATION 国際交流基金
The support from the Japan Foundation for this
publication is gratefully acknowledged.

This book was set in 11-pt. Berling LT Std
by Alpha Design and Composition of Pittsfield, NH.
Designed by Norman E. Tuttle at Alpha Design & Composition

Offset by Avon DataSet Ltd, Arden Court, Alcester, Warwickshire UK
Printed and bound by CPI Group (UK) Ltd, Croydon, CR0 4YY
www.granta.com

More praise for *Earthlings*:

'*Earthlings* is about . . . the freedom to be found when you stop trying, when you abandon all of the rules and indulge entirely in what makes you feel good and comfortable at any cost' *i-D*

'If you loved *Convenience Store Woman* by Sayaka Murata then *Earthlings* will be right up your alley' *Herald*

'*Earthlings* has a similar affectless eeriness to her previous novel, the wildly successful (and brilliant) *Convenience Store Woman*, but where that book was all uncanny control, this one is pure, demented abandon' 'Books of the Year', *Irish Times*

'*Earthlings*' cute cover and conversational tone lull you into a false sense of security, so when the violence comes – and boy, does it come – you're blindsided. For the most part you side with the "aliens" against the machine, but Murata refuses to let it be that simple. Provocative and radical' *Stylist*

'Brilliantly translated by Ginny Tapley Takemori . . . *Earthlings* shares some DNA with *Convenience Store Woman*, with a female central character dealing with feelings of dislocation, but by the end it is altogether weirder and more shocking . . . Murata takes the reader on a journey that is profound and scary in equal measure. Brilliant' *Big Issue*

'As a coded portrait of adolescent anxiety, it's savagely pointed'
Daily Mail

'Unforgettable' *Economist*

'Surreal and darkly comic' *New Statesman*

'Shocking, heartbreaking and very funny – in short, another cult classic from the author of *Convenience Store Woman*' 'Editor's Choice', *Bookseller*

'I loved this book! It easily converted me to being an alien. A radical, hilarious, heartbreaking look at the garbage we have all internalized in order to fit in and survive' Elif Batuman, author of *The Idiot*

'A firecracker of a book. If you appreciate trigger warnings, *Earthlings* requires them all – child abuse, violence, incest, and plenty more. But somehow the story skates along the top of all this darkness, and shimmers with a deadpan wit. I loved it' Cal Flyn, author of *Islands of Abandonment*

'Gut-shredding . . . A frequently disturbing but pacy read, with its own off-key humour. I ripped through it' *Observer*

EARTHLINGS

CHAPTER 1

Deep in the mountains of Akishina where Granny and Grandpa live, fragments of night linger even at midday.

As we wound our way up steep hairpin bends, I gazed out the window at the swaying trees, at the undersides of the leaves so swollen they looked as though they would burst. That was where the pitch-black darkness was. I always felt an urge to reach out to that blackness, the color of outer space.

Next to me, Mom was rubbing my sister's back.

"Are you okay, Kise? These mountain roads are so steep, no wonder you're feeling carsick."

Dad gripped the steering wheel, saying nothing. He was driving slowly to keep the car as steady as he possibly could, glancing anxiously at Kise in the rearview mirror.

I was eleven and in year five of elementary school. I could take care of myself. Looking out of the window at the fragments of the universe was the best way to avoid getting carsick. I'd worked that out when I was eight and hadn't been sick on this road since. My sister was two years older than me, but she was still just a child and wouldn't survive the journey without Mom's help.

As we drove up and up around endless bends, ears popping, I felt like I was gradually moving toward the sky. Granny's house is high up, close to the universe.

I hugged my backpack to me. Inside it was my origami magic wand and my magical transformation mirror. At the very top of the backpack was my best friend, Piyyut, who gave me these magical objects. Piyyut can't speak human since the evil forces put a spell on him, but he's looking after me so I won't get carsick.

I hadn't told my family, but I was a magician, a real one with actual magical powers. I'd met Piyyut in the supermarket by the station when I was six and had just started elementary school. He was right on the edge of the soft toy display and looked as though he was about to be thrown out. I bought him with the money I'd received at New Year's. Piyyut was the one who'd given me my magical objects and powers. He was from Planet Popinpobopia. The Magic Police had found out that Earth was facing a crisis and had sent him on a mission to save our planet. Since then I'd been using the powers he'd given me to protect the Earth.

The only other person who knew my secret was my cousin Yuu. I was dying to see him again. I hadn't heard his voice for a whole year. We only ever got to see each other in the summer when our extended family gathered for the annual Obon festival.

I was wearing my favorite T-shirt, the indigo-blue one with stars on it. I'd bought it with my New Year's money and put it in the closet, still with the price tag on, keeping it especially for today.

"Hold on tight," Dad said quietly as we approached a particularly sharp bend. The car lurched as we went around it. My sister grunted and covered her mouth with her hand.

"Open the window to let in some fresh air," Mom said, and instantly Dad opened the front window on my side. A warm breeze caressed my cheeks, and the car filled with the smell of leaves.

"Kise? Are you okay?" Mom sounded like she was about to cry.

Dad turned off the air-conditioning. "Only one more bend," he said.

I instinctively clutched the front of my T-shirt. I could just make out the slight swellings beneath my bra. They hadn't been there last year. Had I changed a lot since then? Yuu was the same age as me. What would he think?

We would soon reach Granny's house. My boyfriend was waiting for me there. My skin grew hot at the thought, and I leaned forward into the breeze.

* * *

Cousin Yuu was my boyfriend.

When had I started to feel this way about him? Even before we got together, I'd always been drawn to him. We'd been inseparable during the Obon vacation every summer, and even after Obon was over and Yuu went home to Yamagata and I went back to Chiba, his presence never faded within me. In my memory the traces he left grew stronger and stronger, and by the time I was really longing for him it was summer again.

We were nine years old, in year three of elementary school, when we first formally promised ourselves to each other. Our uncles had dammed the shallow river by the rice fields with stones to make a knee-deep pool where we cousins could splash about in our bathing suits.

"Ouch!" I cried as I lost my footing and fell on my butt.

"Careful, Natsuki. The river flows fastest in the middle," Yuu said, his face serious as he helped me up.

I'd learned that in school, but I hadn't made the connection with this little river. "I've had enough of water," I said. "I'm going to play somewhere else."

I climbed onto the riverbank, picked up the small shoulder bag I'd placed carefully on a rock, and put on my beach sandals. Without waiting, I went up the steps to the road and, still in my bathing suit, headed for the house. The bag felt alive, warmed by the sun's rays. As I walked alongside the rice fields, I heard footsteps and knew Yuu was following me.

"Natsuki, wait for me!"

"Leave me alone!" I snapped.

Yuu reached out, picked some small leaves, and popped them into his mouth.

I couldn't believe my eyes. "Yuu, you can't eat that! You'll get a stomachache."

"Don't worry. It's edible. It's called sour dock. Uncle Teruyoshi told me."

He held some out to me. I took them and hesitantly put them in my mouth.

"Ugh, it's so sour!"

"Yeah, it is a bit, but it's good."

"Where did you find it?"

"There's lots growing around here."

We walked around the slope behind the house gathering sour dock leaves, then sat down next to each other to eat them.

My bathing suit was wet and uncomfortable, but I liked the taste of the leaves. Now that my mood had improved, I said, "Since you showed me something you like, to say thank you I'll let you in on a secret."

"What secret?"

"Well, actually I'm a magician. I have a transformation mirror and a magic wand."

"What sort of magic can you do?"

"All kinds! The best spell helps you defeat enemies."

"Enemies?"

"I mean, maybe ordinary people can't see them, but there are lots of enemies all around us. Bad magic, monsters, that sort of thing. I'm always doing battle with them to protect the Earth."

I took Piyyut out of my bag. He looked like a white hedgehog plush toy, but actually he was an emissary sent by the Magic Police on Planet Popinpobopia. Piyyut had given me the magic wand and mirror to help me use my magical powers, I explained.

"Wow, Natsuki, that's amazing!" Yuu said, his face serious. "It's thanks to you protecting the Earth that we're living in peace."

"Right."

"Hey. What sort of place is that Planet Popinpo—what's it called again?"

"Popinpobopia. I don't know really. Piyyut said it was secret."

"Oh."

I thought it was weird that Yuu seemed more interested in the alien planet than my magical powers, and I looked at him closely. "Why do you ask?"

"Um . . . well, don't tell anyone else, but I have a secret too. I'm an alien."

"What?!" I exclaimed, taken aback.

"Mitsuko is always saying so," he went on with a serious tone. "You're an alien, she says. You were abandoned by a spaceship, and I took you in."

"Wow, really?"

Mitsuko was Yuu's mom. She was Dad's little sister, and so I called her Aunt Mitsuko. She was really pretty. She was shy and quiet, just like Yuu. I couldn't imagine she would lie or joke about something like this.

"You know what else? In my drawer there's a stone that I don't remember having picked up anywhere. It's black, flat, smooth, and a really weird shape. So I think it must have come from the same place I'm from."

"Wow. So I'm a magician, and you're an alien!"

"Well, I don't have any proof. Not like you, Natsuki."

"But I'm sure it's true. Maybe you're actually from Planet Popinpobopia. Wouldn't that be amazing? You might be from the same planet as Piyyut!" I said excitedly, leaning forward.

"I wonder. If so, I want to go back home someday."

I was so shocked I almost dropped my mirror. "What?"

"Every time I come here for Obon, I'm always secretly looking for the spaceship that will come and take me home. But I've never found it. I wonder if Piyyut can arrange for it to come and get me?"

"No way, Piyyut can't do that sort of thing!" I felt like crying. I couldn't bear the thought of Yuu not being around. "Yuu, are you going to go away sometime?"

"Probably. I think it would be better for Mitsuko if I did, anyway. After all I'm just an alien that she took in, not her real son."

I burst into tears.

"Natsuki, don't cry," he said and rubbed my back, trying to console me.

"But I like you. I don't want you to go away."

"But they'll come to get me sometime or other I think. I've been waiting for the spaceship for ages."

Yuu's words made me cry even harder.

"I'm sorry, Natsuki. But while I'm still here on Earth, I'll do anything for you. I feel calm when I'm here at Granny's house. I think it's because it's closer to space, so it's nearer to home for me, but it's also because you're here too."

"Really? Then I want you to be my boyfriend until you go back to your own planet."

Yuu nodded. "Sure."

"Really? You mean it?"

"Yes. I really like you, too, Natsuki."

We hooked pinkies and made three promises.

1. Yuu won't tell anyone that I'm a magician.
2. I won't tell anyone that Yuu's an alien from outer space.
3. We won't fall in love with anyone else, even after summer's over. We'll definitely meet up here again next summer.

Just then I heard footsteps. Hastily I hid Piyyut and the mirror inside my bag. It was Uncle Teruyoshi.

"So this is where you got to! I thought you'd been washed away by the river."

Uncle Teruyoshi was always cheerful and played a lot with us children.

"Sorry," we apologized.

He smiled and stroked our heads. "Oh, you got some sour dock! Do you like it, Natsuki? It's quite sour but tasty."

"Yes, I do like it."

"You do? That means you're a real mountain woman now, then! All right, come along. Granny's looking for you because she's cut up some peaches."

"Okay."

We headed back to the house together.

I could still feel where my pinky had hooked Yuu's. I ran to the front door, hoping no one would notice I was blushing. Yuu, too, was walking fast and looking down at his feet.

Ever since then, Yuu has been my boyfriend. The magician would be the girlfriend of the alien, at least until he traveled back to his home planet.

Granny's house opened onto a huge hallway, which was easily as big as my bedroom at home. I always felt a bit lost going inside.

"We're here!" Mom called loudly. Dad, as usual, remained silent.

It smelled of fruit, a mix of peaches and grapes, along with a faint animal odor. The neighbors kept cows, but they were some distance away, so maybe the animal smell in this house came from us humans.

"Oh, come on in! It's hot today, isn't it?"

The shoji slid open, and an older woman, probably an aunt, came out into the hall. I thought I remembered having seen her before, but I wasn't sure. We only came here once a year for Obon, and I had trouble telling the various adults apart.

"Kise, Natsuki, you've gotten so big!"

"Oh, you brought gifts. You really shouldn't have! Sorry you went to all that trouble."

"You remember Natsuko? She's done her back in and can't come this year."

As Mom greeted the gaggle of vaguely familiar middle-aged ladies one by one, they all started chatting excitedly. This was going to take ages I thought, sighing quietly. The ladies had now gotten down on their hands and knees and were bowing to each other. Dad stood vacantly in the entrance.

Granny and Grandpa appeared from the living room, supported by a middle-aged man. Granny bowed to Mom and said, "Thank you for coming all this way."

Grandpa smiled at me and said, "Misako, you've gotten so big!"

"Come on, Grandpa," an aunt said, patting him on the back. "This is Natsuki!"

"You took a long time," Uncle Teruyoshi said cheerfully to Dad as he came out. "Did you run into traffic?"

Uncle Teruyoshi always spent a lot of time with us kids, so I knew him really well. He called out over his shoulder, "Hey you guys! Kise and Natsuki are here!"

Three boys came hesitantly out. These three were Uncle Teruyoshi's sons, my cousins. They were always getting up to mischief, and every year they got told off by the adults. The oldest, Yota, was two years younger than me.

They looked at me and Kise like wary animals. I recognized them all, but they were different from how I remembered. The features on their faces had spread out to the edges, and their noses were more prominent than before. Their bodies had changed too.

I would always recognize my boyfriend, Yuu, of course, but I had a lot of other cousins, and some of them already had their own children, so I felt a little disorientated whenever we met. Even though we all spent every summer here and had a lot of fun together, after a whole year of not seeing each other some distance had always opened up between us again.

The adults were embarrassing us, saying things like: "Hey, no need to get all shy because those two have gotten so pretty." Yota and his brothers looked even more awkward and stand-offish than usual.

"Hello," I ventured. A rather self-conscious chorus of "hel-looo" came back.

"Yuu's here, too, you know." Uncle Teruyoshi said. "He's been asking when you were going to arrive."

Trying hard to keep my cool I asked, "Really? Where is he now?"

"He was doing his homework just over there not long ago."

"Maybe he's up in the attic now? That boy likes it there." This came from Cousin Saki, a tall woman who was much older than me. She was holding a baby. She was the eldest of Aunt Ritsuko's three daughters, all of whom were married. Aunt Ritsuko was Dad's eldest sister.

It was the first time I'd seen this baby. It was kind of weird how a new person that hadn't existed last year had suddenly come into being. The little girl crouching at Saki's feet must be Miwa, who had been a baby just last year.

I couldn't remember all the kids who were close in age to me, let alone my cousins' kids, and had to relearn who everyone was every year. I just followed what Mom did and bowed my head at each new person who appeared.

"Oh, is Mitsuko here?"

"Sure, she's in the kitchen."

"Where's Yuu got to?" Aunt Ritsuko put in. "He's been asking after Natsuki all morning. Maybe he couldn't wait any longer and went off to have a nap."

Uncle Teruyoshi laughed. "Yuu always sticks close to Natsuki, doesn't he?"

They probably said the same thing every year, but considering we were an item now I quietly looked down, feeling embarrassed.

"It's true, the two of them are like twins," another aunt said.

For some reason, everyone said I didn't look like my sister or my parents, but I did look just like Yuu.

"Oh, but you mustn't stand out here in the hall talking. Kise, Natsuki, come inside. You must be tired!" A fat aunt I had absolutely no recollection of ever having seen before said this and clapped her hands.

"Yes, let's go in," Dad said, nodding.

"Go put your luggage upstairs. You can use the far room. The Yamagatas are in the other one. The Fukuokas are already up there, but they're only staying for one more night so you don't mind sharing, do you?"

"Fine by us, thanks," Dad answered, taking off his shoes. I hurried after him.

In Granny's house, everyone called the various families by the name of the place they lived in, like Yamagata or Fukuoka or Chiba, which made it hard for me to remember their real names. They must have had names, though, so why didn't anyone use them?

"Kise, Natsuki, first go greet your ancestors," Dad said.

We headed for the room where the family altar was kept, between the living room and the kitchen. Yuu and I always called this the altar room. There was only one corridor in Granny's house, leading to the bathroom. All the other six rooms on the first floor including the kitchen, living room, and the two main tatami rooms were connected by sliding doors.

The altar room was a modestly sized six-mat room, about the same size as my bedroom back home in Mirai New Town in Chiba. Yota called it the ghosts' room to frighten his little brothers, but somehow I always felt safe there, perhaps because I sensed that my ancestors were watching over me.

Mom and Dad each lit a stick of incense, and my sister and I did the same. We didn't have an altar at home, and I'd never seen them in my friends' houses either. The only times I'd ever smelled incense were here at Granny's house and when we visited temples. I liked the smell.

After lighting her incense stick, my sister suddenly crouched down, her head bowed.

"Kise, is something wrong?"

"Seems she got a bit carsick on the way."

"Oh dear. That mountain road again."

The aunts laughed. One or two of my cousins also joined in, covering their mouths with their hands as they shook with laughter. I had more than ten cousins just on my dad's side. I couldn't remember all their faces. Nobody would notice if an alien slipped in among them.

"Kise, are you okay?" Mom asked as my sister suddenly brought her hand to cover her mouth.

"Dear, dear. You'll feel better once you've thrown up," an aunt said.

"I'm sorry," Mom said, bowing her head in apology, and headed for the toilet hugging my sister close.

"Is that mountain road really all that bad?" asked another aunt. "I mean, how feeble can you get? She could always just walk up if she doesn't like riding in the car."

I felt sorry for my sister. She doesn't have Piyyut like I do. "Don't you think you should go too?" I asked Dad.

"No, she'll be all right," he said, but when he heard her crying he hurried off to help.

I felt better now that she had both Mom and Dad with her.

The phrase "close-knit family," which I'd come across in a school library book and had stuck in my mind, always came back to me whenever I saw my parents and sister together. If I wasn't here, the three of them would make a perfect unit. So I wanted them to spend time together as a close-knit family without me now and then.

Piyyut had taught me the magical power of invisibility. I didn't actually become invisible. I just held my breath and could make myself go unnoticed. When I did this, they became a cozy family of three, all snuggled up together. I sometimes made use of the power for their sake.

"You really like Granny's house, don't you Natsuki?" Mom often said to me. "Kise's like me. She likes the seaside better than the mountains."

Mom didn't like Granny much and wasn't at all pleased by how excited I always got about going to Akishina. My sister always complained about coming to Granny's and clung to Mom at home. So of course she was Mom's favorite.

I picked up my things and headed for the stairs. I felt nervous at the thought that Yuu was up there.

"Are you okay on your own, Natsuki?"

"Sure," I said, hoisting my backpack onto my back as I went up.

The stairs in Granny's house were much steeper than the ones in our house in Chiba. They were practically a ladder, and you had to use your hands to climb them. I always felt like a cat when I went up them.

"Take care!" I heard someone say, an aunt or maybe a cousin. "I will!" I answered without turning around.

Upstairs there was a strong smell of tatami and dust. I went through to the far room and put down my things.

Uncle Teruyoshi told me that long ago this used to be the room where they kept silkworms. Apparently there used to be lots of bamboo baskets packed with eggs, which hatched into larvae that grew rapidly and spread throughout the second floor. By the time they spun their cocoons the whole house was full of them.

I'd seen pictures of silkworms in school library books. As an adult, the worm transformed into a big, white moth, much prettier than any butterfly I'd seen. I'd heard that silk thread was harvested from the worms, but I'd never gotten around to asking how they got the thread and what happened to the silkworms afterward. How magical it must have been to have all those pure-white wings fluttering around the house! It was like something out of a fairy tale, and I loved this room where the baby silkworms had been laid out in rows.

As I slid open the door to leave, I heard the floor creak faintly.

Someone else was up here.

I moved toward the room that everyone called the attic, although it was still on the same level as the rest of the second floor, and slid open the door into the large, pitch-black space. This is where Granny stored all the old toys Dad and my uncles and aunts once played with, along with a large number of books that someone or other had collected. We children always came here to look for treasure.

"Yuu?" I called into the darkness.

Our feet got really dirty when we went into the attic, so we were always being told to make sure to wear the sandals we use to go out onto the veranda, but I was too impatient to fetch them. I just took off my socks before stepping into the darkness.

"Yuu, are you there?"

I headed for a small point of light emanating from a tiny lamp, the only light in the dark room even at midday. There was a rustling, and I almost screamed.

"Who's that?" came a small voice.

"Yuu! It's Natsuki!"

A small white figure appeared indistinctly from the depths.

"Natsuki! Finally!" Yuu was standing there in the faint glow.

I ran over to him. "Yuu! I missed you!"

"Shhh!" he said, hastily putting a hand over my mouth. "We'll be in trouble if Granny or Yota hear us."

"Yeah, true. Our love's still a secret, isn't it?"

Yuu looked at me shyly. He hadn't changed at all in the past year. Maybe it was because he was an alien that he didn't grow. But even in the dark, I could tell it was him from his light brown eyes and thin neck.

"At last we're together again!"

"It's been a whole year, hasn't it, Natsuki. I've been looking forward to seeing you too. Uncle Teruyoshi told me you'd be coming today, so I got up early to wait for you. But he said you'd be late."

"Is that why you're up here playing on your own?"

"Yeah. I got bored."

Yuu hadn't just stopped growing, I had the feeling that he'd even shrunk. Cousin Yota had filled out since last year, but Yuu's neck and wrists looked like they'd gotten even skinnier. Maybe it was just because I'd grown, but he looked so fragile that I couldn't help feeling worried.

I grabbed the edges of his white T-shirt and felt the faint warmth of his body as my fingertips brushed his skin. Maybe it was because he was an alien that his body temperature was low. His hands felt cool as they connected with mine.

"Yuu, are you going to be here for the whole of Obon this year?" I asked, gripping his hands as hard as I could.

Yuu nodded. "Yeah, I will. Mitsuko took a long vacation this year, so she said we could stay."

"Great!"

Yuu called his mom Mitsuko instead of Mom. Apparently she'd told him to. Aunt Mitsuko had divorced three years ago, and since then she'd depended on Yuu as though he were her husband. He said he had to kiss her cheek every night before going to bed, so I'd gotten him to promise to reserve the proper kiss for me.

"What about you, Natsuki?"

"I'll be here all through Obon too!"

"Great! Uncle Teruyoshi bought some big rockets for the fireworks this year. He said we'll let them off on the last night."

"I'm looking forward to the sparklers too!" I said excitedly.

Yuu gave a little smile.

"Will you go looking for the spaceship again this year?"

"Sure, if there's time."

"But you won't go away with the aliens straight away, will you?"

Yuu shook his head. "I won't, I promise. Even if I find it, I'd never leave without saying goodbye to you, Natsuki."

I breathed a sigh of relief. I'd pestered Yuu to take me with him in the spaceship, but he'd said he couldn't. He promised to come back for me sometime, though. He was sweet but strong-willed.

I had the feeling he might disappear at any moment. I wanted to become an alien, too, and I felt jealous of him having somewhere to go home to.

"Yota said he was secretly going to open up the well, without the grown-ups knowing."

"The old well that's been closed up forever? I want to see it!"

"Sure, let's go see it together. And Uncle Teruyoshi said he'd take us to go watch fireflies once it gets dark."

"Brilliant!"

Yuu took everything seriously, and whenever he saw something strange he wanted to know all about it. Uncle Teruyoshi loved telling us about this house and the village, and he ended up spending more time with Yuu than anyone else.

"Yuu! Natsuki! Come downstairs and have some of this cold watermelon," an aunt called.

"Let's go."

Yuu and I left the attic still holding hands.

"Afterward let's go play together, Natsuki."

"Yes, let's."

I nodded, feeling myself blush. I was so happy to be with my boyfriend again.

Dad was one of six siblings, and the extended family gathering for Obon was always madness. We couldn't all fit in the living room at once, so the sliding doors between the two large tatami rooms at the end of the house had been removed, and a long, low table was set up with cushions on the floor for our meals.

The house was full of bugs, but nobody made a big deal of it. Back home in Chiba even a small fly would cause panic, but Mom and my sister never made a fuss about the insects in Granny's house. The boys would eagerly run around killing them with a flyswatter, but even so there were still always flies and grasshoppers and bugs I'd never seen before crawling around the room.

All the girls old enough to help went to the kitchen to make dinner. Even my sister was quietly peeling potatoes.

I was put in charge of dishing up the rice. There were two rice cookers sitting side by side. I filled bowl after bowl as six-year-old Ami, the daughter of one of my cousins, put them onto a tray and carried them through to the long table in the tatami room, helped by Cousin Mari.

"First lot of rice coming up! Make way, please!"

Cousin Mari slid open the kitchen door, and she and Ami went past the family altar to where the uncles were sitting around one end of the table waiting.

"Stop daydreaming and get that rice served!" Mom yelled at me from where she stood tending the pans on the stove.

"Oh, come now, Natsuki's doing a great job," Granny said, glancing over at me as she cut slices of a stinky seaweed jelly that I hated.

"That child is hopeless. She can't do anything properly. I get tired just watching her. It gets on my nerves. Yuri, on the other hand, is doing so well, though. She's already in junior high, isn't she?"

I was used to Mom saying I was hopeless. And she was right, I really was a dead loss. The rice I dished up just lay flat in the bowl instead of being nicely mounded.

"Look how messy that is! Just let Yuri take over. Such a clumsy child." Mom sighed.

"That's not true! She's doing very well!" an aunt said, flattering me.

I carried on serving the rice as best I could, hoping nobody else would call me a loser.

"That red bowl is Uncle Teruyoshi's, so be sure to give him lots, okay?" my aunt told me. I piled on as much as the bowl would hold.

"It's already dark," someone said. "Not long now before we have to go welcome the ancestors."

"They'll soon be lighting the bonfire to guide them to us."

I thought I'd better hurry up and quickly reached for the next bowl.

"Hey, we're going to light the fire now!" Uncle Teruyoshi called from the front door.

"Oh, it's time! Natsuki, we'll deal with this. Off you go, now!"

"Okay!" I said, handing my aunt the rice scoop as I stood up.

I could hear insects chirring outside. Darkness had fallen, and the world beyond the kitchen window was now the color of outer space.

* * *

All of us children followed Uncle Teruyoshi. At the river he would light the fire to welcome the spirits of our ancestors on their annual visit home for the Obon festival.

Yuu was carrying an unlit paper lantern, and I had a flashlight.

The Akishina mountains were in darkness. The river we'd been splashing around in last summer was now so black it felt as though it would swallow us up. As Uncle Teruyoshi set fire to a bundle of straw on the riverbank, our faces glowed orange in its light. We did as Uncle told us and faced the flames.

"Dear Ancestors, please use this fire to guide you to us," Uncle Teruyoshi said.

"Dear Ancestors, please use this fire to guide you to us!" we all shouted in unison.

As we stared at the burning straw, Uncle Teruyoshi said, "Right then, they must be here by now. Light the lantern, Yota."

When he said they were here, little Ami let out a strangled shriek.

"You mustn't shout," Uncle told her. "You'll startle them."

I gulped.

The flame was gently transferred from the straw to the lantern. Yota picked it up and staggered slightly as he cautiously carried it to the house, obeying Uncle Teruyoshi's warning not to let the fire go out.

"Uncle, are the ancestors inside that fire?" I asked Uncle Teruyoshi.

He nodded. "That's right. The fire guided them to us."

As Yota carried the lantern onto the veranda and into the tatami room, the aunts came out to greet us.

"Careful now . . ."

"Make sure it doesn't go out!"

At their urging, Yota proceeded through to the end of the room where an altar had been set up specially for Obon.

Uncle Teruyoshi lit a candle from the flame in the lantern. On the altar were a cucumber and an eggplant, each with four legs made from disposable chopsticks. These represented the horse to bring the ancestral spirits quickly back home and the cow to slow their return to the other world, making them stay longer in the living world. Ami and Yuri had made them that afternoon, knowing the ancestors were on their way.

"There we are," he said. "The spirits of our ancestors are now here around the flame. Natsuki, when the candle burns down, be sure to replace it, okay? Make sure the flame doesn't go out. Otherwise the ancestors won't have anything to guide them, and they'll be in trouble."

"Okay," I said.

I looked at the table and saw that Dad and my uncles had taken their seats and were already drinking sake, while the women rushed around preparing food and serving it up.

My sister and I sat with the other children. On the table in front of us were large serving dishes of edible wild greens and stewed vegetables.

"I want a hamburger!" Yota said loudly, and Uncle Teruyoshi slapped him on the head.

A grasshopper hopped past a plate of soy-simmered locusts on the table.

"Yota, get rid of that."

Yota deftly caught the grasshopper in both hands and went to put it outside.

"Don't be silly! If you open the screen, lots of bugs will come in."

"Okay, I'll go feed it to a spider, then," I said, standing up and taking the live grasshopper from Yota. I took it to the kitchen and gently stuck it on a cobweb. It offered no fierce resistance, just fluttered its wings slightly and became tangled in the spider's silk.

"What a treat for the spider," said Yuu behind me.

"I wonder if it can eat something this big?"

The spider looked taken aback by the huge prey suddenly caught in its web.

We went back to the table and started eating the locusts. I wondered whether the spider had started eating the grasshopper yet and felt a bit queasy. Still, the locusts were sweet and crispy. I shoved another one in my mouth.

As the night wore on, the house became enveloped in the noisy chirring of insects. Some of the children were snoring, but the creatures outside were a lot louder than we humans.

If you left a light on, however dim, bugs would flock to the window screens, so the rooms were kept in absolute darkness. As I normally slept with a lamp on, I felt a little scared and clutched the quilt close to me. The thought of Yuu sleeping just the other side of the sliding doors calmed me.

Nonhuman lives jostled up against the window. The presence of nonhuman creatures was stronger at night. Strangely enough, though I was a little scared, I felt as though my own feral cells were throbbing.

The next morning my sister threw a tantrum.

"I want to go home!" she screamed. "I hate it here!! I want to go back to Chiba NOW!!!"

Kise didn't get on with the other kids in her school. I'd heard from Kanae, whose sister was in the same year, that she'd been dubbed Miss Neanderthal for being so hairy. I wasn't at the same school as her, but even so I'd been asked, "Hey, you're Miss Neanderthal's little sister, aren't you?"

Often I'd be ready to leave for school before Kise had even emerged from her room. More and more she ended up not going to school at all. She stayed home being comforted by Mom instead.

The summer vacation should have been a welcome break for her, but then Yota had asked an aunt why Kise had a moustache. When the other cousins heard about it they all traipsed in at breakfast to see it for themselves, and she'd flown into a rage.

"Look what happens when you tease girls, Yota. Apologize right now!" an aunt scolded him. He did, but my sister wasn't impressed.

"Oh dear. She sometimes has fits, too, doesn't she?" the aunt said, a worried look on her face.

Kise clung to Mom and wouldn't let go. When she got stressed out she usually threw up. For the rest of the day, she kept complaining, "I don't feel well. I want to go home!" And by evening, Mom gave in.

"It's no good. I think she's got a fever. Let's go home."

"I suppose we'd better if she isn't well," Dad agreed.

"Cousin Kise, I'm sorry. I really am," Yota kept repeating. He was on the verge of tears, but she wasn't having any of it.

"You shouldn't spoil her so much," Uncle Takahiro said, and Uncle Teruyoshi chimed in with a soothing voice, "Don't be in such a hurry. The air's fresher here, and she'll feel better after a good sleep. Won't you, Kise?" But Kise refused to back down, and Mom was at the end of her tether.

"We're going back in the morning," she informed me, and all I could do was nod.

Yuu and I had arranged to meet the next morning at six o'clock outside the old storehouse.

"Where are we going?"

"To the graves."

Yuu looked taken aback. "What are we going to do there?"

"Yuu, I've got to go back home today. Listen, I have to ask you something. Will you marry me? Please?"

"Marry you?" he repeated, flustered by my sudden proposal.

"We're not going to be able to see each other until next year. If you marry me now, Yuu, I'll manage somehow until then. Please?"

Seeing how desperate I was, he seemed to make up his mind. "Okay, Natsuki, let's get married."

We sneaked out of the house and headed for the family graveyard in the rice fields.

When we got there, I took Piyyut out of my shoulder bag and put him next to the offerings.

"Piyyut will be the pastor."

"I wonder if the spirits will punish us for doing this?"

"I'm sure our ancestors won't be angry at two people who love each other getting married."

Since Piyyut can't speak human, I recited the wedding vows on his behalf. "Swearing on our ancestors, we hereby marry. Yuu Sasamoto, will you take Natsuki Sasamoto as your wife and promise to love her in sickness and in health, in happy times and sad times, as long as you live?"

Then I added in a small voice "Promise, Yuu."

"Yes, I do."

"Good. Now Natsuki Sasamoto, will you take Yuu Sasamoto as your husband and promise to love him in sickness and in health, in happy times and sad times, as long as you live? . . . Yes, I do."

I took two rings I'd made out of wire from my bag.

"Yuu, put this on my finger."

"Okay." His skin was cold as he slipped the ring onto my third finger.

"Now I'll put on yours." I carefully slipped the other ring onto Yuu's white finger, taking care not to hurt him. "Now we are married."

"Wow. We're man and wife!"

"That's right. We're not boyfriend and girlfriend anymore. We're a married couple. That means we're still family even when we're apart."

Yuu looked a little bashful. "Mitsuko's a bit crazy, and when she gets angry she always says she'll throw me out of the house. I'm really happy I've got a new family now."

"Should we make some more promises? Like we did when you agreed to be my boyfriend. Now we're married we should do it properly this time."

"Okay."

I took out my notebook and started writing with my pink pen.

Marriage Pledge

We hereby pledge the following:

1) *Don't hold hands with anyone else.*

"What about in folk dance?"

"That's okay. Just don't hold hands with another girl when you're on your own."

"Okay," Yuu said, giving me an odd look.

2) *Wear your ring when you go to sleep.*

"This ring?"

"Yes. Look, last night I put a spell on them. So even when we're apart, we can hold hands when we're asleep. At night, we can look at these rings and remember each other, and that way we'll feel reassured and be able to sleep."

"Right."

"And what else? Is there anything you want to add, Yuu? Something we should pledge for our marriage?"

Yuu thought a moment, then picked up the pink pen and wrote in small, neat letters:

3) *Survive, whatever it takes.*

"What do you mean?"

"I want us both to stay safe so we can meet again next summer. I want us to promise that we will do whatever it takes to survive and be in good spirits when we meet up again next year."

"Okay."

We decided that Yuu would look after the piece of paper the pledge was written on. Mom and Kise often threw away my things, so I thought it would be safer with him.

"Make sure you don't break our pledge, okay? And definitely come back here next summer!"

"I will."

We each hid our ring in a pocket and hurried back to Granny's house. As we went in the front door we could smell the miso soup cooking for breakfast.

"Yuu! Natsuki! You're up early!" Granny exclaimed in surprise.

"Yes, I was looking for flowers for my independent study project," I said, giving the excuse I had prepared.

"What a good girl you are!" Granny said, impressed. "Oh, I almost forgot," she said and rushed back to the living room, where she took out some money wrapped in tissues from her bag. "This is for you, Natsuki. It's not much, but you can buy yourself a nice toy with it."

"Thank you!"

"And here's something for you, too, Yuu."

During Obon, the adults always gave the kids some money in an envelope or wrapped in a tissue. We had to tell Mom how much we were given, but it was ours to keep.

I put it carefully into my bag. I was saving up to visit Yuu in Yamagata sometime.

"Oh, you're up already. Good," Mom said as she came down the stairs. "We'll be on our way straight after breakfast. Go and get yourself ready to leave. We have to get back quickly and find a doctor for your sister. It's a holiday, so we'll need an emergency clinic."

"Okay."

Mom bowed to Granny. "I'm so sorry. We really did want to stay until the end of Obon."

"Don't worry. Kise's always been rather frail, hasn't she?"

I looked at Yuu. I wasn't going to be able to stay until the last night of Obon. I would miss the fireworks when we saw the ancestors back on their way to the other world. Hadn't Dad said something about a bus coming up the mountain once a day or something?

"Mom, couldn't I stay a bit longer and go home by bus?" I ventured timidly.

Mom looked at me, her face tired. "Oh do shut up. Go and get ready now. You know very well that it's impossible to calm your sister down once she starts a tantrum."

"But there's—"

"That's enough. Don't you start giving me trouble too!"

"I'm sorry."

I shouldn't get in the way of my "family" anymore. I was married now, after all. I had already left my family, so Dad, Mom, and my sister could finally be a close-knit threesome.

At the thought that Yuu and I were now married, strength welled up in me. I glanced at him. He returned my look and gave a slight nod.

Please let us definitely meet up again safely next year, I thought, mustering all my magical powers to make the wish come true.

Floorboards creaking here and there signaled that morning had fully arrived in the house. In the pale sky visible from the veranda there was no trace of the color of outer space.

* * *

The car was filled with the smell of melted rubber.

"Open the window and let in some fresh air," Mom said, rubbing my sister's back.

I was in the front passenger seat, gazing out the window at the increasingly flat and populated landscape.

Dad had not uttered a word for miles. Mom was desperately trying to soothe my sister.

"Family" is hard work I thought. I gripped the ring in my pocket.

I closed my eyes and conjured up Yuu. Now in the darkness behind my eyelids there were some glimmers of light, like stars. Maybe this was a new magical power, letting me see into outer space where Yuu's home, Planet Popinpobopia, was located.

If he ever found the spaceship, I would get him to take me with him. Now that we were married, I would be going home as his bride. Of course I would take Piyyut with me too.

With my eyes closed, drifting in space, it felt as though the spaceship from Planet Popinpobopia really was close by.

I was immersed in my love for Yuu and my magical powers. As long as I was here in this space, I was safe and nobody could destroy our happiness.

CHAPTER 2

My town is a factory for the production of human babies. People live in nests packed closely together. It's just like the silkworm room in Granny's house. The nests are lined up neatly in rows, and each contains a breeding pair of male and female humans and their babies. The breeding pairs raise their young inside their nests. I live in one of these nests too.

The Baby Factory produces humans connected by flesh and blood. Eventually we children will also leave the factory and be shipped out.

Once shipped out, male and female humans are trained how to take food back to their own nests. They become society's tools, receive money from other humans, and purchase food. Eventually these young humans also form breeding pairs, coop themselves up in new nests, and manufacture more babies.

This was how I'd always thought it was, and when they gave us sex education classes at the beginning of fifth grade, I felt vindicated. My womb was a factory component and would couple with someone's testes, which were also a factory component, in order to produce babies. Males and females all crawled around their nests with these factory components hidden within their bodies.

I was now married to Yuu, but being an alien he probably couldn't make babies. If we couldn't find his spaceship, society would make me form a breeding pair with someone else.

I hoped we would find the spaceship before that happened.

Piyyut was asleep in the bed I'd made for him in my study desk drawer. I continued to use the magic wand and mirror he'd secretly given me. My magical powers helped me take my life forward into the future.

As soon as we arrived home, I called my best friend, Shizuka. She had stayed in town during the Obon holiday and had apparently been bored while I was away.

"So are you coming to the pool tomorrow, Natsuki? I said I'd go with Rika and Emi, but I don't like Rika. It'll be so much more fun if you come too. Let's go on the water slide together!"

"Sorry, but I got my period last night."

"Oh no, that sucks! Oh well, let's go to eat crepes the day after tomorrow, then."

"Sure!"

"Cram school starts next week, right? I hate it, but I'm kind of looking forward to seeing Mr. Igasaki. He's such a babe!"

I laughed. I was enjoying chatting on the phone with Shizuka after so long. Suddenly I felt a forceful thump on my back.

"Get off the phone!"

I turned to see my sister standing there looking cross. I supposed she'd kicked me again. She always comes and kicks my back when I'm on the phone.

"Sorry, it seems my sister wants to use the phone."

"Oh really? Okay then, see you the day after tomorrow!"

"See you!"

When I hung up, my sister said irritably, "My fever comes back whenever I hear you speaking so loudly."

"Sorry."

She pushed me out of the room and slammed the door. It would be ages before she came out. It was always the same.

I tiptoed to my room, trying not to make a sound.

I slipped my ring onto my finger and gazed at it. When I did this, I felt like Yuu and I were sharing the same finger. Come to think of it, my ring finger did look strangely pale. It resembled Yuu's slim fingers I thought, and I stroked it gently.

I lay down to sleep still wearing my ring. When I closed my eyes, I could see outer space.

I wanted to return to that pitch-blackness as soon as I could. I'd never been to Planet Popinpobopia, but I was beginning to feel it was my true home.

The day cram school started, I wondered what I should wear and eventually settled on a black shirt. I buttoned it up all the way to the top. It was a bit hot, even though it was short sleeved.

I picked up my school bag, slipped Piyyut inside it, and went downstairs. Mom was in the hall. She scowled when she saw me.

"What do you think you're wearing? You look like you're going to a funeral."

"Um."

"You're so gloomy, I swear." She sighed. "I'm tired enough as it is."

It's handy having a dumpster in the house. In this house, that's my role. When Dad and Mom and Kise get so fed up they can't bear it any longer, they dump everything onto me.

Mom was just on her way next door to pass on the neighborhood news circular, so I went out with her.

"Hi Natsuki, off to cram school are we?" the next-door neighbor called out to me. "You're all grown-up now!"

"Oh no she isn't," Mom said loudly behind me. "She's always making a mess of everything. Can't take my eyes off her for a moment."

"I don't believe that, eh, Natsuki?" the woman said, turning to me.

"No, Mom's right," I said.

When I wasn't using my magical powers, I really was a dead loss. I'd always been clumsy and ugly. From the perspective of the people in this Baby Factory town, my very presence must be a nuisance.

"In comparison," Mom went on loudly, "your little Chika is so talented. This child is so stupid and slow at doing whatever she's asked. She's like a weight around my neck. I swear I'm quite worn out."

She smacked me on the head with the file containing the circular. She often hit me on the head. She said that since I was so stupid, giving my head a little shock would make it better. And what's more, since it was empty it made a good sound. That was probably true. The thwap as it hit my head rang out loud and clear.

"And just look at how she dresses! What a disgrace. We'll never be able to get her married off looking like that."

I nodded. "Yes, it's true."

The person who had given birth to me said I was a dead loss, so I decided it really must be true. I was probably causing a nuisance to the neighbors just by existing. My sister said I gave her the creeps. I was such a useless lump that she felt stressed out just looking at me.

"I'm sorry," I said, automatically bowing my head in apology.

"Oh, but no! No, it's not the case at all," the woman said, taken aback.

"Well, I have to go," I said, bowing my head again, and I got on my bicycle and headed off to cram school.

"I mean really," I heard Mom's voice behind me. "Where on earth does that child get it from? She doesn't take after us, that's for sure."

As I cycled past the rows of identical houses, I thought to myself again how much like nests they looked. They resembled a huge cocoon that Yuu and I had once found in the Akishina mountains.

My town was a collection of nests, a factory for manufacturing babies. I was a tool for the town's good, in two senses.

Firstly, I had to study hard to become a work tool.

Secondly, I had to be a good girl, so that I could become a reproductive organ for the town.

I would probably be a failure on both counts, I thought.

The cram school occupied the second floor of a community center built in the station area two years ago.

There were two classrooms: the one at the far end was taught by the school's principal. It was for students who were taking exams to go on to junior high school. The nearest classroom was the ordinary course for kids like me who weren't taking an exam. The teacher for this class was a university student called Mr. Igasaki who worked there part-time.

I parked my bike, took off my shoes by the entrance, and went upstairs to the classroom to find everyone else was already seated. Shizuka waved me over, and I sat down next to her.

Everyone looked a little different from when I'd seen them before the start of the summer break. Many were suntanned or had had their hair cut.

"Natsuki, are you going to the fireworks display? You'll wear yukata, won't you?"

"Yes, that's what I'm thinking."

"Shall we go look at new ones together? I saw one with a really cute goldfish pattern."

Everyone was enjoying the summer vacation, but it was still really fun to spend time with classmates again. The classroom was buzzing with the incessant chattering and laughing of twenty or so children.

"Quiet now, everyone!" The door opened, and Mr. Igasaki came in.

"Yay!" Shizuka said happily.

Mr. Igasaki looked just like a member of a popular boys' band, so all the girls loved him. And not only was he good-looking, but also his classes were known for being easy to follow and interesting.

"Natsuki, I have to make some more printouts after class. Will you stay behind to help me?"

"Yes."

Mr. Igasaki was always asking me to help him with things. That day, too, when Shizuka said goodbye a little jealously, I was again left alone in the classroom with him.

"You're doing so much better at social studies now, Natsuki," Mr. Igasaki said.

"Yes," I said and nodded. I really wanted to improve my capability as a "work tool," so I was studying hard.

He stroked my head. Even after he removed his hand, my skin still prickled under my hair.

"Your posture is really bad, Natsuki," he said. His hand came up inside the hem of my shirt and rubbed my back directly on my skin. "See, that's how you sit up straight. If you don't do that, you'll end up getting stiff shoulders, you know."

"Yes." I stretched my back as much as I could trying to get away from his hand.

"There, that's much better. Now hold your belly button in too." His hand started moving around to the front, and I hastily twisted my body away. "What's wrong? I'm trying to teach you how to have a good posture, right? I can't do that unless you behave."

"Yes."

His hand brushed over my bra. I sat rigidly upright not saying anything.

"There, that's better."

Finally he took his hand away, but the tension didn't leave my body.

I was just leaving to go home when he said, "Natsuki, you know, you should wear white knickers, not dark pink ones. Boys shouldn't see them, and they shouldn't show through your clothes either."

"Okay."

I picked up my bag and pedaled my bicycle as fast as I could to get home.

Mr. Igasaki often warned me about the color of my underwear. That's why I wore a black shirt, but it seemed that still wasn't good enough.

It's really hard to put into words things that are just a little bit not okay.

I had the feeling that Mr. Igasaki was a little bit not okay.

I'd been in his class since going up to the fifth grade and starting the regular course at the cram school, and he'd always been like that.

But maybe I was imagining it. It was unlikely anyone as good-looking as him would be interested in an elementary schoolgirl like me. I was probably just being uptight.

I caught sight of someone waving as I sped along on my bicycle.

When I looked closer, I saw that it was Miss Shinozuka, my homeroom teacher.

"Good evening, Miss Shinozuka."

"Oh, Natsuki, how come you're out so late?"

"I'm on my way home from cram school."

"Oh, I suppose that's okay, then."

Miss Shinozuka was middle-aged, and everyone called her the Raving Mad Hag because her chin jutted out and she was always getting hysterical and going on and on. She was a bit like my sister in the way everyone laughed at her behind her back.

"Oh, and by the way, Natsuki, I've just been doing the grading, and you did really well on the last test."

"I did? Really?"

"You never used to be very good at arithmetic, did you? But you did very well this time."

I was pleased. Miss Shinozuka might be prone to hysterical outbursts, but when you got good marks she was really kind.

"You're slow doing sums, but if you just take your time and avoid making silly mistakes, your marks will improve, you know."

"Thank you, Miss Shinozuka!"

Miss Shinozuka rarely got thanked by pupils. When I thanked her so eagerly she responded cheerfully, "Being studious is a good thing, you know."

I had never been given any affirmation at home, so I was hungry for praise. When I was complimented, even on a whim by a hysterical teacher, my chest grew hot, and for some reason I felt like crying.

I wanted to study harder and become the sort of child that grown-ups found useful. Then, even if I was worthless, maybe I wouldn't be thrown out. I didn't know how to live in the wild, so if I was kicked out I would inevitably die of hunger.

"I'll try even harder!" I said fervently.

Miss Shinozuka looked a bit taken aback. "Well, yes, it is good to try your best," she said and then waved goodbye. "You take care now."

Everyone also called Miss Shinozuka an ugly old spinster who'd missed the boat. There was a rumor that she fancied Mr. Akimoto, the sports teacher—as if he would take interest in someone like her, they sneered.

Grown-ups had it tough, too, I thought. Miss Shinozuka functioned well enough as one of society's tools, but maybe she wasn't functioning properly as one of society's reproductive organs.

She was in the position of educating me and ruled over me, but at the same time she herself was also being judged as a tool of society. But at least once you were able to buy food for yourself, you didn't need to worry about being thrown away.

I set off for home once again. In my bag I had a new homework printout. I wanted to finish it quickly, study harder, and get closer to being once of society's components.

I sat in my bedroom looking at the calendar. Today was the last day of summer vacation. On the calendar I'd noted "347 days to go."

Only eighteen days had passed since we'd welcomed the ancestors for Obon. I wouldn't be able to see Yuu again for 347 days.

Our love kept me going. When I thought of the bond between us, it was as though I was anesthetized. I didn't feel any pain.

I wished I were an alien, like Yuu. Yuu and I were the same in that we were both living as parasites on our families, but I couldn't even say I was an alien.

I sat down at my desk and started studying. I wanted to be able to buy my own food as soon as possible. To achieve that aim I would do whatever society required of me.

When I went through to the living room, Mom looked exhausted.

"Mom, shall I make dinner tonight?"

"No," she answered without even turning around. "Don't go poking your nose in where you're not wanted."

"But you look so tired. We learned how to make curry at—"

"I said no. If you start meddling, you'll just end up making more work for me. Try and be a good girl now."

She was right. I was being pushy. From my family's perspective I was worthless, so it was presumptuous of me to try to do anything positive. It took all my effort just to remain at my zero level without becoming a minus.

"You're always the same, all talk, even though you can't do anything."

Mom always told me off when she was irritable. She wasn't telling me off for my own good but because she needed a punching bag. By hitting me with her words not her hands, she regained her composure.

Mom had a part-time job, and she was fulfilling her role as one of society's reproductive organs by raising me and my sister. Of course such a worthy person as her would get tired!

"Our entire family has to put up with you," she muttered to me, and I supposed she was right.

I clenched my fists. This was a magical power I had recently learned. By gripping my thumbs, I could make darkness inside my hands. If I did it well, I could make the darkness inside my hands so black that it was almost the color of outer space.

I liked looking at the universe inside my hands. If I got really good at it I thought, I could teach Yuu how to do it next summer.

"What are you grinning at now? You're disgusting!" Mom shouted.

It was dumpster time.

I went back to my room. The sooner I could stop being a hindrance and become a useful tool for society, the better. If I learned lots of magical powers, maybe I could even be of some benefit to society.

I opened up my magical transformation mirror and looked at myself. After concentrating a while, I got the feeling that I'd managed to transform just a little.

Suddenly I felt invincible. I stood up, went over to my desk, and focused on my homework.

Maybe because of my magical power, the work went fast. It felt as though there was a glow emanating from within my hand as it gripped the pencil.

* * *

Soon enough it was April, and I moved up to the sixth grade. Summer was steadily approaching. My calendar countdown of the days until I could see Yuu was finally down to two digits. I was elated at the thought I'd be seeing him again soon.

My sister asked me to go buy her some stuff from the drugstore where Mom worked. I was looking for eyedrops for my sister's sty when I caught sight of Mom at the far end of the store. She wasn't a qualified pharmacist. She just did things like shelf stocking.

I was just about to go over to ask her where to find the eyedrops, when a young woman behind the cash register shouted, "Not those, Mrs. Sasamoto! You're supposed to be doing the shampoos." Mom pulled an irritable face and headed to the back of the store.

"Godzilla Sasamoto's such a pain in the neck," the woman muttered.

I started. For a moment I thought she was referring to me.

"Yeah, what a grouch. Blows up at the slightest thing. Such a drag," another young woman counting money at the other cash register said with a sigh.

Oh, so it was Mom they were talking about.

So my sister was Miss Neanderthal and Mom was Godzilla. Was it to do with their mother-daughter blood connection, I wondered.

I ended up rushing out of the store without buying the eyedrops. When I turned back to look, Mom was just coming back out into the store in a foul mood. She really did look as though she could explode at any moment.

It was the end of the class, and I was just about to leave when Mr. Igasaki called me back.

It had been quite some time since he'd last done that. We hadn't been alone just the two of us at all since I'd entered sixth grade, and I'd begun to wonder whether I'd mistaken his intentions. I felt ashamed of having been so paranoid.

I followed him back into the empty classroom.

"I wanted to ask you about this," he said and placed something on top of his desk.

It was a small white package wrapped in toilet tissue.

At first I didn't know what it was. When I looked closer, I saw blood and realized that it was a sanitary napkin. The pink wings were familiar.

"Natsuki, you threw this away in the bathroom earlier."

I was speechless.

It was true. I was on my period. I had gone to the girls' restroom during the break and had thrown a napkin away in the triangular corner bin in the toilet. How had Mr. Igasaki known it was mine?

"As a teacher in this school, Natsuki, it is my job to teach my pupils about this sort of thing alongside regular lessons.

You haven't disposed of this properly. Look, some blood has seeped through here, see? You have to wrap it better. I'll show you how to do it."

He wrapped my sanitary napkin in some tissue paper that was on the desk.

"Look, if you do it like this it stays clean. That's better for the cleaners, isn't it?"

"Yes . . ."

"Okay, now you do it."

"What?"

He smiled at me gently, as always. "You can practice it now. I'll watch and make sure you're doing it right."

"Uh . . . now?"

"Yes, you have a fresh one with you, don't you? Change the one you're wearing."

I stood there unable to speak.

"It's like I always say in class, isn't it," he said encouragingly. "Whenever you learn something new, you have to practice it! This is just the same. Is there anything strange about that?"

"No, but—"

"Come on, hurry up and do it before the next class starts. The junior high school students will be coming in soon," he urged me.

I slowly took my pouch out of my bag. Raising my skirt, I pulled down my knickers, doing my best not to let him see anything. They were the beige knickers I used when I had my period.

With trembling fingers I pulled the napkin off my knickers and wrapped it in the tissue paper on the teacher's desk,
then put a fresh napkin on my knickers.

"There, that's much better."

I stiffened, thinking he was about to stroke my head.

I put the used napkin into my pouch and said, "Thank
you," bowing my head to avoid his hand.

"You're a good, obedient girl, Natsuki. Children like you
can be good at studying. Make sure you listen well to what I
tell you."

"Yes."

"Well, then, I'll see you next week. The math homework
is a bit tough, but if you don't understand something you can
ask for my help anytime."

I nodded and fled the classroom.

*Magical powers. I have to summon my magical powers. The power
of darkness, the power of wind—any magical power will do, but
I need something. I have to use my magical powers on my whole
body before my heart feels anything.*

I ran into the house and washed my hands.

The napkin I had just placed between my legs was twisted.
Blood was pouring out of my body. I felt as though I was being
watched by Mr. Igasaki.

"What's up with you? Not even saying hello when you
come home," Mom said, coming over to me.

I didn't know what to say and swallowed my words.

"Oh look, you have a bruise on your knee. Did you bump into something on your bike?" Mom said, unusually gently. She bent down looking anxious.

Maybe if I try telling her now, I thought.

I needed magic to summon my courage. Silently I chanted a spell, then opened my trembling lips.

"Mom, I . . . the teacher . . ."

"What about the teacher?"

"Mr. Igasaki at cram school, he's weird. He has been for a long time, but today he was really weird."

"What do you mean by 'weird'?"

"Well, he's touched my body before now, to correct my posture he said. And today he told me off for the way I use sanitary napkins."

Lines appeared between Mom's eyebrows, and her mood began to turn ugly. "What are you talking about? You only get told off because you do something wrong."

"No, it's not that. He's weird. Strange. Like . . . not normal. When he corrected my posture he didn't just touch my back, he touched my breasts too."

Somehow I just couldn't properly explain the atmosphere Mr. Igasaki had about him when he was being weird.

"You've always had bad posture. I'm constantly warning you about it too. I can't believe you're making out your teacher's a pervert just because he told you off. You've got some nerve!"

"No, honestly, he *was* being weird."

"Of course he wasn't. It's not as if a teacher would take any interest in a child with an undeveloped body like yours. It's only because you've got a filthy mind that you would think that. You're the dirty one, not him," she spat, and suddenly I couldn't get any more words to come out. "Where did you learn about that sort of thing? What a horrible child. You should be using your time to study, not thinking about things like that!"

I felt something burst on top of my head. Mom stood glaring at me with a slipper in her hand.

"Answer your mother!"

"Okay."

Mom had never hit me really seriously like that before. I felt a switch inside me click off. I couldn't feel anything in my heart. The pain had gone, as if I was under anesthetic.

"You totally flunked that last test of yours, didn't you? I swear that head of yours is empty. Isn't it? *Isn't it?*"

She thwacked me on the head with the slipper again.

"Yes, you're right. I'm sorry."

My mouth kept repeating the words Mom wanted over and over like a spell.

Yes, you're right. I'm sorry. Yes, you're right. I'm sorry. Yes, you're right. I'm sorry. Yes, you're right. I'm sorry. Yes, you're right. I'm sorry. Yes, you're right. I'm sorry. Yes, you're right. I'm sorry. Yes, you're right. I'm sorry. Yes, you're right. I'm sorry. Yes, you're right. I'm sorry. Yes, you're right. I'm sorry. Yes, you're right. I'm sorry. Yes, you're right. I'm sorry. Yes, you're right. I'm sorry. Yes, you're right. I'm sorry. Yes, you're right. I'm sorry. Yes, you're right. I'm sorry. Yes, you're right. I'm sorry.

Please don't throw me out. I'll listen and obey whatever you say, just please don't throw me out. A child thrown out by adults will die. Please don't kill me.

The words tumbled wretchedly from my mouth over and over, deliriously, like a spell, an incantation.

I must use my magical powers to stay alive. I must become empty. I must obey.

The homework from cram school was stuffed into my bag at my feet. Yes, I had to get on with studying. I had to study hard, become the sort of child that pleased adults and eventually the sort of adult that pleased other adults.

Mom had gotten herself so worked up she kept hitting me with the slipper, on my face, on my head, on my neck, on my back. The switch in my heart was off, so I didn't feel anything. I held my breath waiting for time to pass. I shut myself up in a pod, like a time capsule in the earth, and held myself absolutely still, barely managing to take my life forward into the future.

How far into the future would I need to take my life so that I would be able to survive?

3) *Survive, whatever it takes.*

The pledge I'd made with Yuu was seared into the fiber of my being.

How long did I have to survive for? Would I ever be able to live without constantly trying to survive?

Looking at Mom, looking at Mrs. Shinozaki, I couldn't imagine it. The thought I would have to struggle for an eternity made me dizzy.

Still, I had to become a factory component as quickly as possible. I had to develop my brain and grow my body to help the society I was being raised in. For now, I held my breath, trying to carry my own life into a future that was just a few hours away, the future when Mom finally calmed down.

After school, I said I was going to play with Shizuka and went out.

Here in the faintly glowing town, outer space was far away. But it would soon be the summer vacation. Just thirty days until I would see Yuu.

I used a telephone card to call him from a public phone. If Aunt Mitsuko answered, I would hang up immediately.

"Hello, Sasamoto here." It was Yuu's voice.

"Yuu! Yuu, it's me."

"Natsuki?" It sounded like a hiccup, he was so surprised.

"Yuu, listen. An alien from your planet came to my place a short while ago." I gripped the receiver. "Piyyut finally managed to break the curse and spoke to me in human. He secretly summoned someone from Planet Popinpobopia to my room in the middle of the night."

On the other end of the line, there was only a light rustling sound indicating Yuu's presence. I plowed on feverishly.

"He said your spaceship is now in Akishina, Yuu. Last time we were looking for it up on the mountain, right? But that's not where it is. Remember Uncle telling us about that small shrine? I haven't ever been there, either, but that's where it is, so let's go looking for it this summer."

"Natsuki, calm down. Is something up? Who told you that?"

"You see, an alien came, and he has to go back right away, but he's from the same planet as you, and he knows about you. So I had to tell you about the spaceship right away. And two people can get on the spaceship. So you can take me with you he said."

Yuu took a deep breath. "I see, sorry I asked. I was just so surprised. Wow. So this summer we'll be able to go back home."

I didn't know how much of what I was saying was true. I had the feeling that an alien had actually come. I also had the feeling it was all my imagination. If it wasn't true, Yuu would be disappointed. But I couldn't help rushing on.

"Yeah, so remember to say goodbye to your friends at school at the end of the first semester. Because we're going home, both of us."

"All right. You too, Natsuki, be sure to say goodbye to your friends and pack your bags so you're ready. There probably isn't much room in the spaceship, but maybe we should take some games."

"We don't need things like that. I never get bored when I'm talking with you."

The sky was tinged a pale black, like washed-out ink. Unlike in Akishina, the night here was too light to hide me. I couldn't wait for the Obon holiday to come, so I could finally get back to night that was pitch-black. I closed my eyes, longing for the darkness of Akishina. Inside my eyes, points shone brightly like a starry sky.

When the summer vacation finally started, I was elated.

Just one week to go until Obon.

The neighborhood association always held its summer festival in the yard of our elementary school around this time. I dressed up in my yukata with a wind chime design and went to find Shizuka. I found her eating shaved ice. She was wearing the yukata with a goldfish design that we had chosen together last year.

"Look, there's Mr. Igasaki!" she suddenly exclaimed.

Startled, I gripped my stick of cotton candy.

"Come on, let's go say hello."

"Wait! No, better not. I saw Rika over there. You don't get on with her. Quick, this way."

I hurried off in the opposite direction. Shizuka chased after me, calling, "Hey, wait!"

Later, I was leaning on the wall of the gym waiting for Shizuka. She had gone to the restroom, saying her tummy felt cold after eating too much shaved ice.

I was just thinking that she was taking a long time when someone grabbed hold of my wrist.

"Good evening, Natsuki."

I suppressed a scream and bowed meekly. "Oh, good evening, Mr. Igasaki."

He looked as though he was wearing white face powder, he was so pale, and his hand was sticky with sweat. I broke out in goosebumps at the sight of his symmetrical, doll-like face—the one Shizuka raved about as being so handsome. Instinctively, I held my arm over the front of my yukata.

"Shizuka already came out of the bathroom and is at my place now."

"What?"

"She started feeling faint when she was waiting in line. My house is just over there, so she's resting there now."

"Really?"

Come to think of it Shizuka had said she was on her period today. Surely she wasn't also being taught how to change her napkins? I felt a shiver of horror. I'd better go to her right away. I had to use my magical powers to save my poor friend.

"Come on, Natsuki, hurry up."

I clutched hold of Piyyut, who was hidden in my bag, as Mr. Igasaki yanked me along with him.

Silently I chanted a spell. My magical powers could make me invincible. I would go and help Shizuka.

I told myself this over and over again. Piyyut was always looking out for me.

"In you come, Natsuki," Mr. Igasaki said brightly when we reached his house.

I'd heard that his parents were abroad on business and that he was on his own in the house for the summer.

"Where's Shizuka?"

"Oh, Shizuka? She was already feeling better so has gone on home."

"Oh . . ."

He said it in such a matter-of-fact way that I was ashamed of myself for having made a mistake. I knew he'd lied to me, but he was so confident and didn't seem to feel in the slightest bit guilty.

"You are a considerate friend, aren't you, Natsuki? Do you like tea? I have some nice strawberry-flavor tea. Take a seat on the sofa while I make some."

I sat on the sofa without saying anything and stared at a box of chocolates that was sitting on the coffee table. It was a large box, brand-new, without even one missing. I thought that maybe Shizuka hadn't wanted any either.

"I thought we could have a lesson here in my house today," he said, bringing in some sweet-smelling tea. "Do you understand what a BJ is, Natsuki?"

"A what?"

"A BJ. So you don't know, then? That won't do. Everyone has to do it when they grow up. I'll do you a special favor and teach you about it today."

He was speaking gently, much like he did in class. But for some reason, I felt really scared. Weird alarm bells were ringing in my head. Maybe Mom was right, and it was just my dirty mind. I felt self-conscious and ashamed of myself for feeling afraid of this cheerful teacher.

"Today isn't a cram school day, but I'll give you a special lesson. You mustn't tell the other children about it, okay? It's a special lesson just for you, Natsuki."

"Okay . . ."

He stood up and came to sit next to me on the sofa. I could feel my skin prickling with goosebumps, but I didn't say anything. Whenever Mr. Igasaki was being a bit weird he was very gentle, but somehow I didn't know what he might do to me if I offended him.

He pushed the table with the chocolates on it away with his foot and stroked my back.

"Well, then, kneel down on the carpet, facing the sofa, looking at me. No, no, not that far away. Come here between my knees."

"But—"

He sighed. "Natsuki, if you're so unenthusiastic you'll really make me mad. You said you wanted to study, so I'm specially making time for you outside school hours. You really must study properly, you know?"

"Okay. I'm sorry."

I didn't recall having told him I wanted to study, but seeing how annoyed he was, I thought maybe I had said something of the sort to him at some point after all. I was scared of making him any angrier, so I meekly obeyed.

"Right. Now, close your eyes and open your mouth. Keep it open and don't use your teeth."

Terrified, I opened my mouth about a centimeter, but he stuck his thick fingers in and opened it to about the same width as when I went to the dentist. After opening my mouth, he wrapped his fingers around my neck.

"Okay? You have to do what I say and study properly. If you don't study hard, you'll make me angry. You don't want that, do you, Natsuki? You're a serious student, after all."

I nodded desperately, my mouth still open.

If I defied an adult, I would be killed. If the adults threw me out, I would die.

Survive, whatever it takes.

The pledge I'd made with Yuu coiled itself around my body like a talisman.

Something warm and slimy entered my mouth. It tasted slightly bitter and had a fishy smell. I desperately kept my teeth hidden. I was terrified of what he might do to me if I disobeyed him and carelessly bared my teeth. He still had his thick fingers around my neck.

With my eyes firmly closed, I didn't know exactly what he was doing to me. I opened my eyes a little and saw he had raised his buttocks slightly from the sofa and moved his groin up against me and was making a strange motion I had never seen before. I felt even more scared and closed my eyes tight again.

He was breathing heavily, and the warm damp wind coming from his mouth curled around my face and the top of my head.

Suddenly some kind of warm liquid spread through my mouth. I thought maybe he'd peed in my mouth, and immediately I felt like throwing up, but the hands on my neck moved to the back of my head, immobilizing me.

Somehow I managed to twist my body and turn my face away, and I vomited the stuff out. What was spattered over the floor was not pee or blood but a strange liquid that looked like yogurt.

"Natsuki, you have to swallow it properly. Like this!" He grabbed the back of my head again.

Suddenly my vision crumpled. Before I knew it, I had left my body and was looking down from the ceiling at Mr. Igasaki holding my head.

Wow, I must have summoned a super strong magical power. I had no idea how, since I hadn't used my wand or mirror. But despite this spectacular magic, I felt no emotion whatsoever and simply watched my own body in silence from the ceiling.

Seeing Mr. Igasaki holding my skull and using my head as a tool, I vaguely understood. I'd thought I wasn't yet a fully fledged member of the Factory, but actually I was already one of its tools after all.

Mr. Igasaki was talking to my body, which was now empty since I was up on the ceiling.

"This lesson has to be repeated many times. I have this house to myself over the summer. I'll hold a summer school course just for you, Natsuki."

"Okay," my body said. Floating in space, I watched abstractedly as my body faced Mr. Igasaki.

"I am doing you a big favor by teaching you this, Natsuki. You understand that, don't you? You mustn't tell anyone. I'm not just your teacher, so if it ever gets known that I've been showing you favoritism and giving special classes, I'll get into trouble. And you will too, Natsuki. You'll get into even more trouble than I will. After all, you pleaded with me to give you these special study sessions, didn't you?"

"Yes."

"Make sure you come back for more study sessions. You can come next Monday, can't you?"

"Yes."

Next week was Obon. I wouldn't be in Tokyo. But my physical body was nodding at him, as my out-of-body self on the ceiling stared down at it, watching.

Afterward I went straight home. Hovering overhead, I watched myself walking toward my house.

I didn't know when I would be able to return to my physical self. All I could do was watch, not thinking about anything.

I saw Mom speaking to me. "So you got lost again," she said, looking exasperated. I felt terribly sleepy and went straight to bed without replying. Still out of my body, I watched over myself as I took off my yukata, put on my pajamas, and went to sleep. The moment my physical body's cheek flopped onto the pillow and fell asleep, my hovering self lost consciousness.

After a long deep sleep, I awoke to find my consciousness had returned to my physical body.

I desperately wanted to have a bath. As I got up I felt the urge to vomit. I rushed to the upstairs toilet, but my stomach was empty, and nothing came out.

Back in my room, I looked around feeling disorientated. My yukata and obi were neatly folded, and my pajama buttons done all the way up. It was just as my hovering self had observed yesterday.

My throat was dry. I recalled having bought some orange juice at the festival and took it out of my bag.

The moment I poured the lukewarm juice into my mouth, I felt something wasn't quite right. It didn't taste of anything. I thought maybe it had gone bad, but when I sniffed it, there was the usual sweet orange smell.

I thought this was strange, but I wanted to brush my teeth and have a bath. I took a change of clothes and went downstairs.

Mom would probably be angry with me since I hadn't answered her yesterday. I wondered what had happened to Shizuka. I felt sick all over and crept toward the bathroom, trying hard not to make any noise.

Just then, I heard voices in the living room.

"I don't want to go to Nagano this year," my sister whined. "I want to go abroad."

"You've been working hard, Kise, haven't you?" Mom said. "I agree. We can't afford to go abroad, but we could probably manage a hot springs resort. I'd prefer that too. We always go to Nagano every year. We could skip it just this once, couldn't we?"

"I guess," Dad said vaguely.

I burst into the room. "Noooooooooooooooo!" I howled. "We're going to Granny's place for Obon! We're going to Akishina! Noooooooooooooooo!"

"Stop being so selfish!" Mom shouted. But I couldn't stop wailing. "Why are you always so self-centered?" She smacked me on my head.

The out-of-body magical power. I had to summon the out-of-body magical power. If I used that, then I wouldn't have to feel anything.

"Really, you only ever think of yourself. Even just yesterday, we thought you were lost but you came home as if nothing had happened and went straight to sleep. You're such a dead loss, you really are."

She kicked my back. She kicked me just the same way my sister did.

However hard I chanted incantations to myself, today I couldn't manage to leave my body.

Mom kept shoving me with the back of her foot.

I was dragged back to my room screaming.

"Don't come out until you've calmed down," Mom spat and went back downstairs.

I took Piyyut out of the drawer where I kept him and crouched down hugging him close to me.

Please let me summon the out-of-body magical power, so I can go to be with Yuu.

I stayed in my room for the rest of the day chanting incantations, not feeling hungry at all.

When night fell, I put the wire ring on my finger and huddled down in bed. I shut my eyes tight and tried to summon darkness, but there wasn't a single star behind my eyelids. I fell asleep looking at the underside of my own skin.

The next morning I woke to find myself being shaken. I opened my eyes a crack. Mom was standing by my bed dressed in black.

"Get ready right away. We're going to Nagano."

"What? Why?"

"Grandpa died. He hadn't been well for a while, but nobody expected him to die suddenly like this."

Had I used black magic instead of white magic, I absently wondered as I lay in bed. Maybe my magic had granted my desperate wish to meet Yuu, come what may.

"Your sister can wear her school uniform, but you'd better wear black. What have you got? Oh, that dress will do. Anyway, hurry up and get ready. We're leaving in an hour.

When we walked in the front door of Granny's house it was completely different from the way it was in summer.

There were large paper lanterns I'd never seen before in the altar room. In the living room, nobody was sitting around; everyone was dressed in black and rushing about.

"We'll just put our bags upstairs, then go greet Grandpa," Dad said.

Normally he was timid and tiptoed around Mom and Kise, but today he was in charge. When he said we had to greet Grandpa, I wondered if maybe he was actually still alive, just very ill, but I couldn't work out how I could ask Dad what he'd meant.

Grandpa was asleep in the altar room. He was lying on a white futon that was softer and fluffier than any I'd ever seen. The faint smell that he'd always had about him hung in the air.

Granny was dressed in black and sat by Grandpa's pillow with tears in her eyes.

"Kise, Natsuki, will you come and greet your grandfather?"

"Okay," I said in a small voice, but Kise remained sullenly silent.

"Come on then. You might be a bit shocked, but you are both big girls now, so you'll be okay. Come and greet him," Dad said, gently turning back the cloth placed over Grandpa's face.

Grandpa looked the same as he always did, only his eyes were closed, and he had cotton wool stuffed up his nose. He was a bit pale but looked as though he might get up at any moment.

"See, isn't he handsome? He even looks like he's smiling," Aunt Natsuko said, wiping her eyes. She had her arm around Granny.

"He looks like he's asleep, doesn't he?" I said in a small voice.

Dad looked at me and nodded. "It was rather sudden, but he passed away peacefully."

"What does pass away peacefully mean?"

"It means he had a gentle and easy death. He lived a long life too. He was in hospital a while, but he didn't suffer and died in his sleep. That's why he looks so peaceful now."

"I see," I responded. "May I touch him, just gently?"

"Sure, go ahead."

I squeezed Grandpa's hand. It was cold and had turned into a thing. He was not a real person anymore.

"I'm scared," said my sister, who had been silent all this time.

"Why's that, Kise? He passed away peacefully, which is a good thing, you know. Well, others are waiting, so let's move on."

I looked behind me and saw Yuri in her school uniform and Ami in a black dress standing in line with tears in their eyes.

I went back to the front door and saw Aunt Mitsuko there with Yuu, who was dressed in a long-sleeved black blazer.

Our eyes met, and Yuu looked closely at me with a worried expression on his face.

Aunt Mitsuko, in floods of tears, was clinging to him. "Mitsuko, are you okay?" Yuu asked her. He looked more like her husband than her son as he rubbed her back.

"The wake will be tonight," Dad said. "And the funeral's tomorrow."

"It was so sudden!" Mom said with a sigh. "There's still some time until evening. You must be tired. Why don't you take a nap?"

"I don't feel well," my sister said and went to lie down, still wearing her uniform.

"What about you, Natsuki?"

I shook my head. I was wide awake, my eyes bright. I could still feel the sensation of Grandpa's lifeless hand on my fingertips.

I noticed Yuu standing in the garden, wearing a black coat. Quietly I slipped away from the bustle of the house and went to his side.

"Yuu."

Hearing my voice, he turned to me. "Natsuki, are you all right?"

His arms and legs had grown, making his face appear smaller. Even so, he was still shorter than me and doll-like.

"What are you doing?"

"I'm picking some flowers from the garden. Have you heard? Grandpa's going to be buried."

I shook my head. "No, I didn't know. What does that mean?"

"He's not going to be cremated. He's going to be buried in the ground."

"Wow, really?"

I recalled having seen funerals in TV dramas where the body was cremated and then everyone picked out bones using special chopsticks. I'd assumed that Grandpa's funeral would be the same, but now I couldn't picture what it would be like at all.

"Granny said he must be feeling lonely now, so we should give him some flowers from the garden."

"I'll help you pick them."

"Maybe you should get some scissors?"

"Yuu, I want to ask you a favor," I said, without looking up. "I probably won't be able to see you again."

"What?" he sputtered, looking at me in surprise. "Has something happened? Are you moving away?"

"Um, you see, I won't be able to come here anymore," I said in a small voice. He stared at me uncomprehendingly. "Yuu, did you find the spaceship?"

After a few moments, he shook his head. "No. I stopped at the shrine on the way here, but it wasn't anywhere to be seen."

"Oh. In that case, we definitely won't make it in time. Look, you and I are married, right? I really don't have time. Please, Yuu, I want you to have sex with me."

"Eh?" His voice came out like a hiccup.

Paying him no attention, I went on, "Please, Yuu. I'm begging you. Before my body stops being mine, I really want to be physically married to you too."

My voice shook. He stared at me in astonishment.

"But that's what grown-ups do, isn't it? It's not possible for us."

"Yuu, have you ever thought that your life doesn't belong to you?"

For a moment he couldn't get his words out, but then he said in a small voice, "Children's lives never belong to them. The grown-ups own us. If your mom abandons you, you won't be able to eat, and you can't go anywhere without help from a grown-up. It's the same for all children." He reached out a hand to cut a flower from the bed. "That's why we have to try hard to survive until we've grown up ourselves."

Yuu's scissors cut through the sunflower stalk. Now a corpse, the sunflower sagged and leaned against him. He caught it as it fell.

"You know what?" I murmured. "It's possible I might be killed. That's why, before I die, I want to marry you. Not just a promise between children, but really married."

Yuu looked at me in surprise. "What's going on, Natsuki? Who's going to kill you?"

"A grown man. Nobody can stop him."

"Isn't there anyone who can help you?"

"Children are powerless against him. He's strong. And the grown-ups are all too busy living their own lives. They won't help a child. You know that, Yuu."

A sunflower petal fell from Yuu's arms as he stood there in silence.

I looked up. "Hey, Yuu, maybe those are edible."

"Eh? What?"

"The sunflower. It's already dry. Maybe we can harvest the seeds." I pointed at the black center of the sunflower.

Granny always sent us sunflower seeds at the end of summer. I often used to eat them at home in the garden when fall arrived.

I stood up and rubbed the drooping sunflower's black face. Small seeds dropped out into my hand.

"Are these the same things Granny always sends us?" Yuu said, peering cautiously at them.

"I think so. Haven't you ever harvested sunflower seeds before?"

"No."

I put one of the seeds in my mouth. "It's still a bit green."

I still couldn't taste anything. I couldn't detect even a hint of the fragrance I always smelled when eating sunflower seeds. I could tell just from the feel in my mouth that the seeds weren't yet dry.

Yuu also hesitantly put a seed into his small mouth. "Yuck, they don't taste of much, do they?"

"They have to dry out more," I said knowingly.

Yuu's mouth moved nervously. "Natsuki. I'm your husband, so I'll do anything for you," he said. "Do you really want to do that? Will it save you?"

"Yeah."

Yuu tilted his head as if he didn't really get it but said okay.

"Really? You really don't mind?"

"No. As your husband, I'll do whatever I can." He gave a little smile.

I looked down at him. He was still smaller than me. "Me too," I said. "As your spouse I'll do whatever I can for you. I'll protect you, Yuu."

"What does spouse mean?"

"You don't know? Um, I guess it's like a partner in life, so . . . we're family," I said, wishing I had a dictionary to look up the proper meaning of "spouse."

Yuu smiled happily. "Oh I see! Because we're husband and wife. That means we're family."

"That's right."

Beneath the sunflowers, Yuu and I furtively held hands. His hand was soft, like a girl's.

* * *

The next morning, I put on my black dress again and went downstairs to find Grandpa lying in a coffin in the big tatami room where we usually all sat around the long table at mealtimes. The aunts and uncles were dressed in mourning clothes. They were kneeling in rows before a priest, who was chanting sutras.

A line of people waited to burn incense at the altar. Once that came to an end, it would finally be time to take the casket out.

Everyone got into position following Uncle Teruyoshi's instructions: those most closely related over there, the eldest son here, and so forth.

"Do you want to help carry the coffin, Yuu?" Yuu gave a small nod. "In which case you come here. Now, Yota, you're more closely related than Yuu, so you'd better come here."

"I want to help carry it too," I said.

Dad looked a bit taken aback.

"But you're a girl, Natsuki," Uncle Takahiro said awkwardly.

"Well, you can just rest your hand on it," Uncle Teruyoshi said. "Come over here."

I did as Uncle Teruyoshi said and went to the back of the coffin.

"Right then, let's get going."

We all filed onto the veranda, slipping on our shoes as we carried the coffin out.

I looked behind me and saw Mom and Kise walking close together. My cousins and aunts had formed a line behind Granny. All dressed in black, they looked like a column of ants.

We carried the coffin on a path through the rice field to the burial ground, the one we always visited at Obon. A rectangular hole had been dug in the soil.

"Who did that?" I asked Dad. I wondered when my uncles could have found the time since they'd been busy until late with the wake. Dad told me that the villagers had all pitched in to help.

We lowered the coffin into the hole.

"Shall we say our last goodbyes, then?" asked Uncle Teruyoshi.

They opened up the coffin. Uncle Takahiro, his voice hoarse, said, "Well old man, you got long in the tooth, didn't you?"

The aunts looked at Grandpa's face and choked up.

Dad peered into the coffin. Then he simply said, "I guess he'll rot quickly in the summer heat."

They closed the casket, and everyone took turns to shovel some earth on top.

I was just thinking that it was going to be a lot of work to bury him when I heard Uncle Teruyoshi say, "Well then, let's go back."

"But we haven't finished filling in the grave. Is it okay?" I asked Dad.

"The villagers will finish it off for us," he told me.

I wondered where all these super-helpful villagers had sprung from, but I just nodded meekly and followed everyone back to the house.

We arrived to find lots of people I'd never seen before helping to prepare the feast. I was surprised by how many people there were in the village. The banquet ended up going on forever.

"When the old man in the house down the road died, the earth didn't fall in for ages, did it?" said Uncle Teruyoshi.

"Right. But when I looked at his grave just now it had."

I didn't understand what they were talking about, so I asked Dad, "What does it mean, the earth falls in?"

"When you bury a body, the earth is mounded up over the top of the grave, right? When the coffin rots away, it collapses and the earth falls in," he explained tersely.

Once the main banquet ended, they closed off the doors between the two main tatami rooms to provide a space for close family members to continue grieving alone while the other guests chatted and slowly dispersed.

"Well then, time for the after-party," Uncle Teruyoshi said jovially.

"Okay, okay," the aunts said and went off to the kitchen to make snacks.

"I guess it's about time to get the prayer beads out," Uncle Teruyoshi said around nine o'clock when everyone other than close family had gone.

We sat together in a circle holding a long string of prayer beads I'd never seen before and rotated it while chanting the Nenbutsu.

By the time we'd finished, everyone was tired. The aunts started getting ready for bed. Even the uncles didn't seem in the mood to drink any more alcohol and had switched to tea.

"You kids must be tired too. Take turns to have your baths, okay?" one aunt said, and my cousins and I all chorused, "We will!"

There wasn't much time, so my sister and I went to the bath together. It had been ages since we'd last done that, and it felt a bit creepy. Kise's breasts and thighs had rounded out. She resembled the ancient Dogu clay figurines I'd seen in a textbook at school. I felt a bit scared and tried not to look at her body as I washed myself. She also averted her eyes.

When we got out of the bath, still not speaking, and went into the corridor, Yuu was standing outside holding his towel.

"The bath's free," I told him.

"Thanks," he said.

Kise went straight upstairs. I went to the living room where the grown-ups were drinking tea and said good night. Then I went upstairs too.

I could hear Kise and my cousins snoring. I lay staring quietly into the darkness.

* * *

"Are you sure nobody saw you?" I whispered to Yuu.

It was two o'clock in the morning. We'd both slipped out of the house. Yuu had been waiting for me beside the store-house half-hidden by flowers, just as we'd agreed.

"Yep. Everyone was asleep, even the uncles."

I was carrying the backpack I'd hidden earlier in a card-board box near the front door. Inside I had a flashlight, but it would be a disaster if the light were seen. We walked as far as the road in the dark, holding hands.

"Maybe it'll be okay now," I said, taking out the flashlight and turning it on.

There were no streetlights. The only light came from the moon and the stars. I shone the flashlight into the pitch-black before our feet.

"Where shall we go?"

"Where we won't be found."

I hadn't realized it would be as dark as this. It was always night when we carried a flame to guide the ancestors at Obon, but those times Uncle Teruyoshi and all the children would be lighting the way with flashlights so it felt completely different. The most our single flashlight could manage was a dim circle of light at our feet, and I couldn't see Yuu's face.

"Which way should we go?"

"Shh. I hear water," Yuu said.

I peeled my ears, and it was true. There was the faint sound of running water.

"Let's go to the river."

We headed toward the sound of the water. We always called it the river, but actually it was just a shallow stream that only came up to your ankles. That same river now sounded so loud.

"Careful you don't fall in."

"You too, Yuu."

I passed the flashlight to Yuu, and we walked close together following the sound of the river.

When I felt we'd walked some distance, I muttered, "Where are we now?"

"I don't know. If I raise the beam up, someone might spot us. Plus, we won't be able to see where we're putting our feet."

"Let me have a try," I said, taking the flashlight from him. I shone it around just a little, but it was like being in a dark hole. I couldn't see a thing. I could tell there were fields planted with fresh green rice, but I couldn't see any kind of landmark I recognized.

"Have we come down the mountain?"

"I don't reckon so. Oh!" Yuu said in a small voice. "We're not far from Grandpa's grave."

"What? No way!"

I thought we'd walked quite a long way, but actually we were near the burial ground in the rice fields where we'd held the ceremony for Grandpa that afternoon.

"What shall we do?"

"Should we go to the grave? I don't know what else there is farther along this way."

"Okay."

We made our way carefully toward the graves along a levee between two paddies.

Next to Grandpa's grave there was a patch of exposed earth. For some reason we held hands. Maybe we were both a bit scared about being in the place where Grandpa's corpse was buried.

With the sound of water and the rustling of the rice plants, it felt like being next to a big dark sea.

"This is where we got married too," Yuu sighed.

"Should we do it here?"

"What? Here?"

"Are you scared?" Although I myself wasn't quite sure what might be so scary.

Yuu thought about it a moment, then answered, "No, I'm with my 'spouse,' so I'm not scared."

We sat down next to each other in a small space next to the grave. I rummaged around in the backpack with the flashlight and brought out a large piece of cloth and a candle I'd found in the attic. I also took out a sex education book that I'd borrowed from the library.

"What's that book?"

"It tells you how to do sex. I borrowed it from the library."

"Oh."

When I took out a mosquito coil, Yuu said in surprise, "You're well prepared, aren't you!"

I placed the candle and the mosquito coil next to each other and lit them with a match. In the dim light, I could finally kind of see Yuu's face. We took our shoes off and stood on the cloth.

"It's a bit like playing house," Yuu muttered.

"Yuu, I get the feeling *I'm* the alien. I want to touch you with my whole body, except my mouth."

"Why not your mouth?"

"Well, you see, my mouth was destroyed recently. So I can't taste anything, and it doesn't belong to me anymore. But everywhere else is still okay. My hands and feet and belly button are all still mine, so I want to touch you with them."

"Okay."

He was used to me saying weird things. He meekly assented without asking anything more about my mouth.

First we tried hugging each other. He smelled of the orange fragrance of the soap in Grandma's bathroom.

"I want to get closer to you, Yuu."

I had a vague idea about sex as "getting closer" to each other.

I nuzzled all the exposed skin of my body against him. His skin was soft, like an entirely different creature to the rough hands of Mr. Igasaki, I thought with relief.

"I want to get even closer," I whispered urgently.

The sounds of insects and frogs was loud enough to drown out my voice. I worried whether Yuu had heard me, but then he responded, "Even though we're this close already?"

I felt reassured. The warm breath he exhaled tickled my shoulder.

"Have you ever had the feeling that you want to get inside someone else's skin?"

"I never thought about it," he said, his face still pressed against my shoulder.

"Can I come closer?" I asked, clinging to him.

Yuu thought a moment, then said, "Yes. You can come as close as you like, Natsuki."

I clung to the shirt inside his parka. Even so, it still felt too distant, so I undid the buttons and rubbed my cheek directly on his skin.

"Do you feel a little closer now?"

I pressed my ear against his chest and heard his heartbeat.

"I can hear your voice coming from inside you."

"Really?"

"Yeah. When you talk, your muscles move, and your voice carries from inside."

"Sounds weird."

Yuu's laugh sounded from inside his skin. Inside his skin his body was making sounds. I desperately wanted to find my way in there.

"I want to get even closer," I murmured deliriously.

"Even more?" he said, sounding a little put out.

I took off my blouse and underwear and clung to him.

"Now I feel a little closer than before."

"I'm glad."

Yuu's body warmth enveloped me. I felt his veins wriggling beneath the soft skin of his wrist.

"I want to meet the Yuu inside here. I want to go inside your skin," I murmured.

"Natsuki, you keep saying that, but how can you get any closer than you already are?"

If we kissed, we could go inside the skin. That's probably why grown-ups kissed. It had never occurred to me that there was such an animal-like meaning in the romantic kisses I'd read about in girls' manga.

But my mouth had already been killed, so I couldn't kiss.

"Can we kiss with anything other than mouths?" I asked.

"How about foreheads? Or cheeks?" he said.

"But wouldn't you have to use your mouth to do that?"

"Oh, right."

Just then another part of Yuu's body where his internal organs were exposed came to mind.

"Yuu, if you put your organ inside my body, I'll be able to get into your skin, won't I?"

"My organ?"

When I explained what I meant, he looked shocked.

"But that's sex, isn't it?"

"Yes. That's why I said from the start that I wanted to do sex."

Even as I said this, I was scared. What if Yuu's penis was dirty like Mr. Igasaki's?

But when he took his clothes off, it looked completely different. It was pale and looked just like a plant sprout. I was relieved.

"If you put that into my body, will I be able to get inside your skin?"

Yuu looked at me questioningly. "I don't know. Is it even possible?" he said nervously.

Together we searched for the organ that was supposed to be between my legs. We somehow found it and together used our hands to part the membrane and open the hole. We slowly stuck Yuu's organ into it.

Then something strange happened.

Even though we were only joined by our organs, I was swimming inside Yuu's body.

"I got there! I'm inside your skin, Yuu!" I murmured, my voice hoarse. Yuu looked as though he was in pain.

Little by little we stopped talking and were just breathing. We were both swimming in each other's bodies. The insects chirred and the grass swayed in time with our breathing.

"I feel like I've come a long way away," I somehow managed to tell him. "I feel like I've come to a really far-off nearby place with you."

Yuu seemed to be drowning inside me. Transparent saliva dripped from his wide-open mouth. I touched the water falling from him.

Ever since I was born I had wanted to come here I thought. I had reached a place that was not Akishina or that white town where I lived or inside a spaceship, but much farther away.

Relief was winning out over pain. Our organs were blending together and making the sound of water. In our bellies, we were quietly eating each other's body heat.

I could hear the rhythmic sound of Yuu snoring. Without realizing, we had both dozed off.

Taking care not to wake him, I quietly sat up. The organ sprouting from Yuu slipped out of me.

I reached a hand into my backpack.

In there was the medicine that I sometimes stole from Mom's bag. The pills she took when she couldn't sleep. I always stole two tablets at a time. I had been collecting them in an empty sherbet candy pack where nobody would find them.

Soon my entire body, not just my mouth, would be killed, and I would become a tool for grown-ups. I had decided some time ago that I would die before I let that happen.

When we left home I had made up my mind to never go back. If I died now, then for my funeral they would probably just open up Grandpa's grave and bury me together with him. That would be far more convenient for the grown-ups than having to dig a new grave or cremate me.

The transparent candy pack was half full of the tablets, which looked just like the original sherbet candies. I shook them out onto my hand and tried to swallow them together with some juice.

"Natsuki?" I heard Yuu say in a small voice. "What did you just put in your mouth?"

Candies, I wanted to say, but my mouth was too full of tablets and juice to answer.

When I turned around, Yuu's face was pale. He stuck his fingers into my mouth and prised some of the tablets out.

"Spit them all out!" he shouted, apparently realizing they weren't candies. "Natsuki, come on! Spit them out! Now!"

I felt him stick his fingers in my mouth again and remove some more of the half-dissolved tablets.

Saliva welled up in my mouth, and when I tried to swallow it he yelled at me furiously, "Don't swallow!"

Terrified, I meekly froze with the saliva still in my mouth.

Yuu passed me the bottle of fruit juice and said harshly, "Wash your mouth out with this, and spit all of it out. Don't swallow even a drop of it."

I took a mouthful of juice, rinsed my mouth out, and spat onto the grass.

"Did you swallow any of it? Even a bit?" he asked me several times, to be sure. I shook my head. "Mitsuko did the same thing one time," he said quietly. "She'd been given medicine by the hospital, and she swallowed it all in one go."

"Aunt Mitsuko did?" I finally managed to say.

Yuu nodded. "That's why I have to become a tool, so that Mitsuko can survive."

"Yuu," I said, my voice breaking. "When will you be able to go back to outer space?"

He looked down. "I probably won't ever be able to go back. I can't find the spaceship no matter how hard I look." His face was covered in the dark night, and I couldn't see it very well. "We have to do whatever it takes to survive, Natsuki."

"Until when?" I muttered, repressing the urge to cry. "How long do we have to just survive? When will we be able to live rather than just focusing on surviving?"

"When we grow up. Then we'll be able to live."

"Really?"

"Definitely."

I felt like saying that Aunt Mitsuko still seemed to be surviving rather than living, but I swallowed my words.

"I want you to promise me you'll survive until then."

"Okay . . . I promise."

Relieved, Yuu looked up. Just then we were blinded by a bright light.

"What do you two think you're doing?" I heard my sister scream.

We huddled together, still naked.

"Over here! Quick!"

There were loud footsteps. Circles of light descended on us.

For some reason I felt absolutely calm. Next to me, Yuu seemed calm too. He narrowed his eyes against the dazzling light but didn't make the slightest movement.

The half-crazed adults came running toward us. "What the . . . What the heck are you doing?" a flustered Uncle Teruyoshi managed to wring out, his voice hoarse.

"Don't you have sex, Uncle?" I said and immediately felt a sharp shock on my cheek. I looked up and realized Dad had hit me.

"Get them back to the house and lock them up!"

Yuu and I were ripped apart, and I was thrown into the storehouse. I briefly caught sight of him by the rice fields being beaten as they dragged him off.

All the aunts and uncles, plus Mom and Dad, were more upset than I'd ever seen them before. I found it all ridiculous.

"Stay here and be quiet for a while!" Dad yelled.

Resisting the urge to burst out laughing, I said, "I'm not the one yelling. It's you and the other grown-ups."

"Don't answer back! You can stay here until morning to calm down. As soon as it's light we're taking you back home."

"Dad, why are you all making such a fuss?"

"*What* did you say?" Mom sputtered behind him.

"What's wrong with me and Yuu having sex?!"

"Because . . . because you're just children!"

"Why shouldn't children have sex? There are plenty of grown-ups who want to have sex with children. So why is it wrong if they're both children?"

"Natsuki!"

Dad hit me on the head. I lost my balance and fell on the storehouse floor, but even then I laughed.

"You're disgusting!" my sister yelled from behind Mom. "You're only kids. And you're cousins too!"

"Natsuki, stay in here and reflect on what you've done," Mom said in an admonishing tone.

"I don't need to reflect on anything. And I'm not scared of the dark either."

Mom shrieked and lunged at me, but Dad restrained her.

"Best lock her up for a while. Maybe by morning she'll have come to her senses."

The door of the storehouse slammed shut, and I was left in the pitch-black. I could hear Mom and Dad's voices outside.

"Why on earth . . . and when the funeral has only just taken place . . ."

"We won't bring her here again. We must never let her see Yuu again."

"I've always thought they were a problem, those two. It's so gross!" my sister's voice rang out loud and clear.

"Natsuki's become rebellious all of a sudden."

"She has bad friends at school. After all, she's not the sort of child to know about that sort of thing."

It was ludicrous. Grown-ups used children to satisfy their sexual desires, yet the very idea of children having sex of their own volition sent them into a total fit. It was laughable. They themselves were just society's tools, after all! But my womb was still all mine. My body would belong to me alone until grown-ups killed me.

"I don't suppose she could be pregnant . . ."

"No way!"

The aunts were up in arms. Actually, I'd be glad if I was. But Yuu probably hadn't yet experienced the "spermarche" we'd learned about at school. His body was completely free of that sticky fluid that had come out of Mr. Igasaki.

The grown-ups, who did what society wanted of them, were shaken by those of us who did not.

The grown-ups had become anesthetized and seemed unable to remember what life had been like before. They all seemed to be under some kind of spell.

I stayed in the dark, unable to sleep until dawn came.

The storehouse door opened, and my parents and sister came in carrying our luggage. They grabbed my arms and stood me up.

"We're going home."

It was just beginning to get light. I wanted to ask where Yuu was, but I knew they'd never tell me.

I was dragged out barefoot, my feet covered with dirt.

"What about my shoes?"

My black loafers were thrown at me without a word.

My thighs and knees were still covered in dirt too. Dad was always really fussy about us being clean when we got in his car, but today he just pushed me in without a word.

Mom and Kise sat either side of me on the back seat. Once the car set off I wouldn't be able to escape, but Mom was gripping my arm anyway, so hard the bone hurt.

The car started. I glanced back at the house. I could see someone standing in the window, but I didn't know who it was.

We drove along the expressway in silence. When my sister said, "I have to go to the bathroom," we pulled into a service area.

"I need to go too."

Mom took me to the toilet and waited outside the door. "Don't get any funny ideas now."

When I went into the cubicle, I took off my left shoe. I was thinking back to when we used to play treasure hunt with Yota and the others. A seashell or pebble would be hidden somewhere in the house and everyone would hunt for it. Yuu was the best at hiding the treasure, and I was number one at finding it.

Ever since I'd put my shoes on that morning, I'd thought that one of them felt funny. I took the insole out. As I'd guessed, there was a treasure from Yuu there. He'd hidden it last night.

Marriage Pledge

We hereby pledge the following:

1) *Don't hold hands with anyone else.*
2) *Wear your ring when you go to sleep.*
3) *Survive, whatever it takes.*

Natsuki Sasamoto
Yuu Sasamoto

It was the pledge we'd made when we got married last year. Yuu had kept it safe. Scribbled in the margin in Yuu's writing was: "Keep your promise, remember!"

With my back to the toilet door, I closed my eyes and crouched down. Behind my eyelids was darkness. The sensation of connecting with Yuu's organ yesterday lingered between my legs.

The back of my eyelids was the same color as the universe in which Yuu and I had together submerged ourselves. I kept staring into the darkness, barely suppressing the urge to cry out.

CHAPTER 3

felt something on my ankle and looked down thinking it was a bug, but it was just the laces of my sneaker. I couldn't be bothered to put down the supermarket bags I was carrying in each hand, so I decided to leave my laces undone and started walking again.

I was on my way back to the condo by the station where I now lived, about a fifteen-minute walk from the house I had grown up in.

I got married three years ago, at the age of thirty-one. My parents had urged me and my husband to rent a condo by the station in Mirai New Town in Chiba where I was born and raised. I had resisted at first since it was inconvenient for commuting into Tokyo and also because I found the lack of change in my life depressing, but now I felt it was convenient in its own way, being located close to the station and supermarket.

I should have bought the mineral water online as I usually did I thought, adjusting my grip on the shopping bags as the plastic handles cut into my palms. I'd seen it was on sale and had picked up two bottles.

The breeze blowing in from the balcony that morning felt chilly so I'd worn a light trench coat, but now I was too hot. The sun was still strong even though it was already almost October.

When I finally got home, my husband was out on the balcony tending to the plants. He peeked his head around the curtain to greet me.

"This one with a thick trunk has gotten pretty dried out."

"You don't need to water that one until spring. I read in a book that when it gets cold, it sheds all its leaves and hibernates, and when spring comes around it puts out new shoots."

"Oh, really? Plants are incredible!"

My husband was a meek guy and easily impressed. He gently touched the trunk with a respectful look, as though he were standing before the bronze statue of some great personage.

"You wouldn't believe what plants are like in Akishina! They're so rampant there you can easily be swallowed up by them. You have to constantly tend to the house and vegetable gardens or they'll immediately succumb to the force of nature."

"I never get tired of hearing about Akishina. It just sounds so amazing! So different from Tokyo. Your stories of your grandparents' house are like a dream. Someday I really want to go there."

He loved it when I talked about Akishina. He came in from the balcony.

"Tell me more!" he said happily. "Oh, I know. Tell me about the silkworm room again."

"Well, I only ever heard about it from my uncle. I never actually saw it myself. But the silkworms were started off in an upstairs room. The room isn't all that big, but according to what my uncle told me, the worms were kept in rows of bamboo baskets in there and fed mulberry leaves. They grew really fast, so before long the whole house would be full of them."

He listened entranced, as though I was telling him a fairy tale. I always ended up feeling as though the stories I'd heard from my uncle were actually my own experiences, and I would get carried away talking about them.

"Oh, and in spring, they would always buy five chicks to raise for eggs, and after two or three years they would wring their necks and eat them at Obon or New Year."

"You must have eaten those chickens at Obon, right, Natsuki?"

"Maybe, but I don't think they kept any chickens at the Akishina house when I was little."

"Oh, it's wonderful, like the gift of life itself! I've only ever seen meat wrapped up in packs in the supermarket. Tokyo's awful. You can't learn any of the things that are important to being human there."

He seemed to have the intense longing for the countryside that was typical of city people. My family never mentioned Akishina, so when he listened so intently to me I felt soothed by nostalgia.

As we chatted, I put a pan of water on to boil.

"What are you eating today?"

"I was thinking of having pasta, but after talking with you, Tomoya, I think I'll have soba noodles instead. My uncle told me that back in Akishina they would boil the chicken with onions and shiitake and things to make soup. That made me think of kamo nanban soba noodles with duck and onion soup."

"Mmm, sounds tasty."

I put one portion of noodles into the pan. We rarely ate together, even on weekends. In that sense, too, it was comfortable having him as a life partner.

For his own meals, he usually bought whatever he felt like eating at the convenience store, like bento or rice balls. He hated his mother's cooking and didn't particularly want to eat anything homemade. When I was tired, I sometimes did the same, but I would often make something quick and easy like noodles.

"I think I'll have a quick nap," he said.

"Go ahead. It is the weekend, after all."

"Okay, then."

I had really wanted to get away from the place I'd grown up in, but the main reason I was glad I was still living here was not the proximity to the station but the cheap rent, which afforded us the luxury of renting a condo large enough to sleep separately, each in our own bedroom.

My husband sleepily drank a glass of cold mineral water from the refrigerator then went to his room. I'd never set foot in there, but I'd caught a glimpse of some shelves of his favorite books and some model figures that had been precious to him since childhood. We both spent a lot of time holed up in our respective rooms, but there was nobody here to harass us about it as there had been when we were little, so it was a pleasant enough existence.

I sat at the table to eat the soba noodles I'd made from my uncle's memories and my imagination. They didn't taste of anything. My husband had left the window open, and a breeze carrying the smell of autumn blew in and fluttered the tablecloth.

My husband was a full-time employee of a family restaurant an hour's commute away in Tokyo, and I was an office temp at a company that rented out construction equipment. My contract had just come to an end, and since I had some savings I was taking my time to find a new job.

If too much time passed it would look bad when I went for interviews, so I was thinking of taking two weeks off at most. Still, I'd had to do a lot of overtime in my old job and was enjoying being able to laze around the house all day.

The only slight annoyance was that a number of my childhood friends still lived in the area. Some were single and living with their parents, but like us others were renting condos aimed at young families near the station, and some had even taken out loans to buy their own place. Hearing them all talk about how much easier it was to find day care nurseries here than in Tokyo and how being close to the grandparents was ideal for bringing up children, I thought idly that our town really was an ideal factory for raising children, just as I'd felt back when I was still in elementary school.

Gossip spread fast through the network of classmates left in the area. As soon as I stopped work, a text came from Shizuka.

Been ages ♫ Bumped into your mom in the mall the other day. She said you're off work at the mo ☆ I left my job too and am working part-time now ~ ♪ I'm free every Tuesday. Come over for lunch sometime?

I just wanted to relax and enjoy my break so I was a bit reluctant to respond, but I wrote back anyway.

Yay, it's been ages! I'd love to ♪ I'll bring cakes ☆

Ever since I was little I'd had the habit of imitating my friends' use of emoji and style when texting. Shizuka never used that many emojis, but she did favor stars and musical notes, so I used them in my answer to her too. I didn't mean anything much by it. I just thought that matching myself to others might help reduce the chances of causing offense if, for example, my words came across as too tense or gloomy or perhaps too curt and cold.

Shizuka lived in a nearby high-rise. We had ended up at different high schools and universities and had lost contact for a long time, but she had gotten back in touch after she married and moved back to the area six years ago.

I wasn't the sort to have many friends, and whenever she texted me I found it annoying but was also kind of relieved. Without her to ground me, I thought, I and my husband could easily be left behind together by society.

We quickly decided on a date, and two days later I rang her doorbell carrying some cakes I'd bought from the mall by the station. She had started wearing even heavier makeup since getting married, but otherwise she hadn't changed much since she was little. She greeted with me with an angelic smile.

"Natsuki, I haven't seen you for *ages*! Come on in!"

She was much flashier than she'd been when we were little I thought as she welcomed me effusively. Taking the cakes from me, she showed me through to the living room.

The baby she had produced was sleeping in its cot in the living room. Shizuka's place always reminded me of the silkworm room in Akishina. The sight of her baby lying here melded in my mind with the rows of baby silkworms in the silkworm room. I had started to think that maybe we, too, were made to breed by a huge invisible hand.

"How have you been?"

"Nothing's particularly changed. Just I'm thinking that for my next temp job, I'll look for something closer to home."

"Definitely a good idea. After all, you'll be thinking of having kids soon, right? Best get a job where you don't have to do much overtime. Otherwise you won't be able to cope with the housework, and you'll be worn out even before you start raising a child."

"In our house, my husband and I both do the housework and clean up after ourselves as much as we can."

When I explained to Shizuka that we even shared the laundry, she sighed.

"That's wonderful. You're so lucky to have a husband who does his share of the housework, Natsuki."

"I guess."

My husband and I each cleaned our own rooms, and in the shared spaces like the living room, kitchen, and bathroom we had a rule that after using them we would return them to their original clean state within twenty-four hours. That way, since we mostly ate our meals separately, we could avoid burdening the other with our own washing up and cleaning. To begin with we'd set the time limit at twelve hours, but I'm the type that likes to go straight to sleep after eating and I couldn't keep up.

It would probably be different if we had children, but it worked well for us to live according to these very simple rules. Shizuka seemed really envious of our situation.

"Your husband sounds like he'll make a great dad, Natsuki."

I laughed.

To avoid Shizuka's inquisitive gaze, I automatically covered my belly with a handkerchief I'd placed on my knees.

She had at times nonchalantly tried to find out whether I was pregnant. If I happened to drink caffeine-free tea or refrained from alcohol, for example, she would immediately pick up on it and say, "I understand, it's normal not to tell anyone until you're sure, isn't it?"

To be certain she wouldn't make the mistake of thinking I was pregnant now, I asked for another espresso. She looked disappointed as she took my cup and headed for the kitchen.

"I might be jumping the gun a bit here, but don't hesitate to tell me if you need help looking for a day care nursery or a good hospital or that sort of thing. That sort of information is so important, isn't it?"

"Thank you. But we haven't any plans at the moment."

"Really? It's not for me to poke my nose into your marriage, but you'd better not leave it too long. A friend of mine currently undergoing infertility treatment said that the hospital she's going to is really good. If you're interested, I'm sure she'll give me the details. There's a good herbal remedy for that kind of thing too," she said, smiling.

Shizuka had changed, but in some ways she hadn't changed at all. She'd grown up, but even now she still believed strongly in society. She had always been exemplary in learning to be a woman, truly a straight-A student. It looked excruciatingly tiring.

When the time came for her to collect her other child from day care, she picked up her baby, and I went back home. I felt rather tired and, without going into our living room, went straight to my bedroom and lay down on the bed.

I'd only been out for lunch and cake in the neighborhood, but I felt strangely exhausted. I decided to change out of my dress so I could sleep and sluggishly got up and opened the closet.

Inside was a tin box. Uncle Teruyoshi had found it in the storehouse when I was little and had given it to me. After taking off my dress, I gently took it out and opened it.

Inside was Piyyut's blackened corpse, the yellowing marriage pledge, and the wire ring.

"Popinpobopia," I murmured in a small voice.

I had the feeling that the ring flashed in response, as if that word were a magic spell.

My life had completely changed after what happened between Yuu and me.

Dad had always been taciturn, but after that incident he stopped talking to me altogether. Mom and my sister took turns to keep watch on me. Even after I went on to college and got a job, I was not allowed to leave home.

When I started working as a temp after leaving college, I'd said I'd wanted to live alone, but Dad had refused. "I never know what you'll get up to without anyone to keep an eye on you," he said, not looking at me. "It's my duty to ensure you don't bring dishonor on the Sasamoto family name."

I was still expected to become a component for the Factory. It was like a never-ending jail sentence. I thought I probably wouldn't ever be able to be an effective Factory component. My body was still broken, and even after becoming an adult I wasn't able to have sex.

In the spring three years ago, when I'd just turned thirty-one, I registered on surinuke dot com. As its name suggested, this was a site where people seeking to evade society's gaze for some reason, such as marriage, suicide, or debts, could appeal for information or find collaborators. I went to the MARRIAGE page and checked the category for NO SEX • NO CHILDREN • REGISTERED MARRIAGE to search for a partner.

> Thirty-year-old male, Tokyo resident, urgently seeks marriage partner to escape family surveillance. Businesslike arrangement with all housework shared, separate finances, and separate bedrooms preferred. Absolutely no sexual activity, and preferably no physical contact beyond a handshake. Someone who refrains from showing bare skin in shared spaces preferred.

Quite a few men checked the box for NO SEX, but this one had caught my eye for having stipulated especially detailed

rules. I'd be marrying a complete stranger on the verbal promise of no sex, so the less anxiety a potential partner provoked
in me the better. I immediately sent him a message, and after
meeting two or three times in a café, we came to a mutual
agreement and tied the knot.

My husband was heterosexual, but he'd had to bathe
together with his mother until the age of fifteen and simply
couldn't handle a real woman's body. He did have sexual ap-
petites but he could satisfy them with fiction and wanted to
avoid seeing female flesh as much as possible. I never asked
him for details, but from what he'd told me his father was
extremely strict. If by getting married he could get them off
his back, he would be grateful.

When we lodged our marriage papers at city hall, my
parents and sister were so delighted it was almost creepy. Neither my husband nor I had many friends, and I didn't want to
see my relatives after what had happened, so we didn't hold
a ceremony. My sister strongly recommended we take a com-
memorative photo at least, but we decided against that too.

My husband had an elder brother, but they didn't get
along very well. In that respect, too, our family environments
were similar. It made things easier.

I'd hoped that after my marriage I'd be able to leave the
area I'd grown up in, but due to my parents' strong wishes
and the fact that it would have been astronomically expensive
to rent a two-bedroom place in Tokyo, we chose this condo
near the Mirai New Town station. My sister had also tried to

persuade us to buy a place instead of renting, but we rejected that idea.

Life with my husband was pleasant in its own way. We ate our meals separately. If there were any leftovers we sometimes shared them. We also washed our clothes and underwear separately, me on Saturday, he on Sunday. We each washed our own towels, and we would do the shared items like the curtains, toilet mats, and so forth together on a day off once every few months or so. We took turns to clean the toilet every weekend. There were lots of rules, but as long as we kept to them it meant we didn't have to do anything bothersome. Once I got used to the arrangement, I found it comfortable.

I was extremely relieved about his insistence on absolutely no sexual contact. He was more neurotic about it than I was. The loungewear I'd previously worn at home exposed my calves, which revolted him, so I started wearing a tracksuit instead. We hadn't even so much as shaken hands. At most our fingertips had brushed handing over a parcel.

I'd always vaguely assumed that I would automatically become a Factory component when I grew up, but this didn't happen, and with this arrangement we really did slip past the gaze of relatives and friends and others who lived in the neighborhood.

Everyone believed in the Factory. Everyone was brainwashed by the Factory and did as they were told. They all used their reproductive organs for the Factory and did their jobs for the sake of the Factory. My husband and I were people they'd

failed to brainwash, and anyone who remained unbrainwashed
had to keep up an act in order to avoid being eliminated by
the Factory.

I once asked my husband why he'd registered at surinuke
dot com. "I thought it was written into our contract not to pry
into that," he said, clearly uncomfortable.

"I'm sorry, that was out of order. I didn't mean to infringe
on our contract."

"No, it's okay. I feel surprisingly relaxed talking with you,
Natsuki."

It wasn't that my husband had no interest in sex. Instead
he thought it wasn't something to do but rather something to
observe. He enjoyed watching, but he was apparently disgusted
by the notion of touching or being touched by someone who
was discharging fluid. Another problem my husband had was
that he hated working. This was obvious in his behavior at
work, so he found it hard to hold a job down.

"Deep down everyone hates work and sex, you know.
They're just hypnotized into thinking that they're great." My
husband was always saying that.

His parents, his brother and his wife, and his friends sometimes came to spy on us. My and my husband's womb and
testes were quietly kept under observation by the Factory.
Anyone who didn't manufacture new life—or wasn't obviously
trying to—came under gentle pressure. Couples that hadn't
manufactured new life had to demonstrate their contribution
to the Factory through their work.

My husband and I were living quietly in a corner of the Factory, keeping our heads down.

Before I knew it, I had turned thirty-four, and twenty-three years had passed since that night with Yuu. Even after all this time, I still wasn't living my life so much as simply surviving.

Early the following week my husband was fired from his seventh job.

"I can't believe that company flouted the labor standards law so blatantly. I'll get my revenge, just you wait!"

He couldn't handle alcohol so he was guzzling Coke, shaking with rage. He had often felt uncomfortable at work and changed jobs of his own volition, but this was the first time he'd been fired. I was surprised too.

It appeared he'd been caught using money from the safe at the restaurant he'd been working at for the past year to play pachinko. After he told me about this, I thought it was hardly surprising he'd been fired. I was just glad the police hadn't been involved.

"But all I did was invest money to make more out of it, then gave it back! What's wrong with using the store's money to do that? It's so unfair."

"Anyone who breaks the rules in the Factory is harshly judged. It can't be helped. You'll just have to find another job."

My husband threw himself down on the sofa, pushing his face into a cushion. "Dad's going to be on my back every day again now. I want to go somewhere far away!"

"Keep quiet about the pachinko and come up with a good excuse for why you took the money. I'll back you up."

"I want to die!"

"What are you saying?"

"No really, I do want to die. First I want to experience freedom from the Factory, just once, and then I want to die."

I wanted to stop him, but I couldn't think of any good reason why I should make him stay in this world. If only there was something he liked or wanted to do, but there just wasn't. Yet he continued to survive, and so did I. If I asked myself what I was surviving for, I couldn't really say.

"I want to go somewhere far away before I die. Oh, I know. I'd love to go to the house in Akishina that you're always talking about, Natsuki. I'm sure it must be even more beautiful and amazing than I can imagine," he said, captivated.

I was taken aback. All my childish stories had built up Akishina into a kind of Shangri-la for my husband.

"Well, that house is really a long way away, and it belongs to my uncle now, so it'd be difficult for us to go there."

"I guess. And it's nothing to do with me, after all. But for some reason I feel more longing for that place than any other I've been to. I'd like to try sour dock once in my life before I die." He closed his eyes as if his soul had already flown off to Akishina.

"Shall I go visit my parents this weekend and sound Mom out about it?" I asked, in spite of myself. "But my cousin's apparently living there at the moment, so I think it'll be absolutely out of the question. Anyway, don't get your hopes up. If by any chance my cousin's already moved out, it might be possible to stay there for a couple of days."

"Really?"

"Look, I think it's probably impossible. But I can ask. And even if we can't go to the house, maybe we could visit the area and stay at an inn."

"Wow, it would be totally amazing to actually go to Akishina! I want to stay in the silkworm room and go into the attic too! And I want to go down to the river where you used to light the fire to greet your ancestors. Oh, if I could even just go to see those mountains, it'd be such a lifesaver!"

"Hey look, I'm really not sure it can happen, you know. Long ago there was some trouble between my family and our relatives," I explained, seeing he was getting his hopes up. Still, if it made him that happy, I thought, perhaps we might be allowed to stay in a local inn and go for walks, even if it was impossible to stay at the house.

My husband had been white as a sheet, but now his cheeks were flushed as he gesticulated wildly in his excitement. Just seeing him like this took me back to summer vacations at Akishina and how I used to get so excited playing on the veranda.

"You know what? Tomoya's been fired from work, and he's exhausted. He keeps going on about how he wants to spend some time in the countryside," I began nervously that weekend when I saw my parents. It had been a while.

"Oh, the poor darling! Maybe he's all depressed? That is a worry, isn't it?"

Ever since my niece was produced, Mom had started speaking in a gooey sort of drawl.

From the direction of the sofa came the sound of my niece crying. My sister now lived in a condo she'd bought about five stations away and had come visiting today to show off the grandchild.

"And I'll understand if it's impossible, but . . ." I trailed off, unable to fully broach the subject.

"What is impossible?"

"Um, well . . . we're talking of going away for a few days."

"Lucky you. Childless couples have such a leisurely life," my sister said, rubbing my niece's back.

"Kise, really!" Mom chided.

My sister shrugged. "But I think going on a trip would be a good idea too. Don't you, Hana?" My niece recoiled at the face suddenly looming large over her and twisted her body away, clinging to her teddy bear. "My friend couldn't conceive for ages. But when they finally decided to take a vacation to relax together in a holiday villa, she got pregnant right away. It works better being surrounded by nature, you know."

"I suppose so. Maybe it is a good idea. Have you got anywhere in mind?"

I immediately shook my head. "No. But a hot springs resort might be nice. We'd be able to take it easy there."

"Oh, that sounds wonderful," Mom said. "After all, you never did go on a honeymoon, did you? Go and have some fun."

"Okay," I said meekly.

Ever since the scandal with Yuu back when we were still in elementary school, Mom and Dad had never once mentioned the circle of relatives that included him in my presence. Even when my grandmother died when I was fifteen, they'd refused to take me to the funeral, telling me I had to focus on my exams. Later I overheard Kise and Mom saying that Yuu had been there, even though he was in the same year at school as me.

That hadn't changed even after I married three years ago. They had apparently relaxed a tiny bit, since they had on occasion let slip mention of Uncle Teruyoshi or Aunt Mitsuko, and I'd been shocked to learn that Aunt Mitsuko had died years ago. But they never said anything about her son.

My sister sometimes gave me updates about Yuu when my parents were out, dropping comments casually as if to see whether I showed any reaction to his existence. I always tried not to move any facial muscles as I listened. Since my parents never spoke about him at all, ever, anything she said was a precious source of information, even if it was just a test.

According to my sister's gossip, Yuu had lived alone as a college student in Tokyo and had vacated the house in Yamagata when Aunt Mitsuko died. She seemed annoyed that Uncle Teruyoshi had helped him with his college fees, but my heart beat faster at the thought that he was living much closer to me then than he had been over in Yamagata. I was careful to just say "Oh really?" without letting my interest show at all.

When I heard that he'd got a good job working for a men's clothing wholesaler, I recalled how he always studiously finished his homework during summer vacation, never shirking his studies. I wasn't surprised to hear he was a hard worker.

About a year ago I heard from my sister that his company had been acquired by another firm and he had taken voluntary redundancy.

"It's because of the recession, I guess. The severance pay is higher if you leave quickly, apparently, so he volunteered. I guess he was unlucky, but then he was quite shrewd about it too. For the moment he's living in the Akishina house on unemployment benefit."

"In Akishina?" I blurted out, despite myself. Her mention of the place I missed so much caught me off guard.

"Yes! Uncle Teruyoshi has always doted on that boy. Yuu apparently went to him in tears saying he'd always loved Granny's house and wanted to rest his mind and body there for a while. Uncle's such a soft touch I swear. My hunch is that he's secretly planning on settling in and not moving out. That boy brazenly took his inheritance from his estranged father and frittered it away, you know. I really don't know what he's thinking. Aunt Mitsuko was always going on about how he seemed more like an alien than her flesh and blood, and she was right."

"Right," I finally managed to answer, keeping my face down so as not to let her see my expression.

That had been a year ago. Just as my sister had said, Yuu was still unemployed and living in the Akishina house.

Just then the phone rang.

"Oh my, what a long time it's been! Yes, yes . . . What? Akishina you say? Tomoya said that?"

Startled to hear my husband's name, I mouthed "Who is it?" to Mom, who looked bewildered as she gripped the receiver and kept bowing to the person on the other end, even though they couldn't see her.

"Er . . . no, we don't mind at all. Yes, of course."

Mom hung up and turned to me looking bewildered. "That was Tomoya's mother, thanking me for agreeing to let Tomoya stay at the Akishina house. Perhaps you can enlighten me as to what this is all about?"

I couldn't believe my ears. "My mother-in-law said that? Really?"

"You do know that in that house your—"

"I know! Tomoya was saying how much he wanted to go there, but I told him it was impossible."

"So why did I get that call just now?"

"I have no idea! He must have gotten the wrong idea somehow. I'll put him straight when I go home."

My sister cuddled my niece to her and said provocatively, "Oh, but what a great idea. You should go! Akishina is the perfect place for you to go for your honeymoon, isn't it?"

"Kise!" Mom said loudly, but Kise was looking at me unperturbed.

"What's the problem? If it's all right for Yuu to live there, then surely Natsuki also has the right to visit the place too, hasn't she? The cheek of the boy! Even if Uncle Teruyoshi did agree to let him stay there, it's a bit much for him to carry on living there without paying any rent. Really, it'd be best to kick him out, wouldn't it?"

Mom looked nonplussed. "Well, you see, Uncle Teruyoshi inherited that house, so we don't have any right to tell him who he can or can't let stay there."

"Yuu is Aunt Mitsuko's son, so he's nothing to do with Uncle Teruyoshi. Ever since she died, Uncle Teruyoshi has been strangely fond of that boy, but if you ask me Yuu seems to be somehow angling to take over. It's so messed up!"

"Even if he sold the house, he wouldn't get much for it, it's so run-down," Mom said bitterly.

I felt really uncomfortable, but I could hardly just walk out. I stood there unable to move.

It never occurred to me that we'd actually make it to Akishina I thought with a sigh as I sat on the Nagano-bound bullet train watching my husband tuck into his bento.

Of course he'd rashly told his mother about it. He'd been so excited at the possibility of going to Akishina that he'd let it slip.

The network of relatives had been activated with a flurry of phone calls, and Mom and Dad had urgently discussed whether it was really acceptable for us to stay there and whether it would be better to send Yuu somewhere else.

But Dad's eldest sister, Aunt Ritsuko, said that such a long time had passed and now that I had a husband it should be okay, shouldn't it?

"Look, Natsuki, you were just a child. You haven't even been to visit Granny's grave yet, have you, you poor thing? I still think that you should have come to the funeral, too, to say goodbye to Granny, you know. You're all grown up now, so why keep harping on about the past? And you know, hearing the laughter of children around the house was Grandpa's sole joy. Obon was never the same after that. Granny and Grandpa are so lonely in their graves. Just go pay them a visit, won't you, Natsuki?"

Aunt Ritsuko wasn't generally one to intervene in family disputes, but when she did her words carried weight, and even Uncle Teruyoshi couldn't oppose her. Reluctantly, Mom and Dad both agreed to let me and my husband go to Akishina.

"I wish I could get Yuu to go somewhere else, but he's already moved out of his Tokyo apartment, and he doesn't have anywhere to live now. I suppose I could pay for him to go stay a few nights in a hotel, but that seems ridiculous, doesn't it?"

Mom really didn't seem to like Yuu. Even just the mention of his name disgusted her and made her irritable. Dad was much calmer and took a surprisingly cool attitude to it all, saying, "Well, it's a big house, after all. And Tomoya will be there, too, so I'm sure things will be fine."

My husband seemed oblivious to the Sasamoto family's hasty phone discussions. He just sat staring nonchalantly out of the window.

"Oh, I'm so looking forward to it! I'll finally get to go to Akishina! It's like a dream come true."

The only way to get to Akishina from Nagano Station was by bus or car. Since there was only one bus a day, it was decided that Uncle Teruyoshi would come to pick us up.

"I'm sorry to drag him out. If only you or I could drive, Natsuki."

"Even if you could drive, that winding road is nigh on impossible for anyone who isn't used to it. My mom can drive, but she always got my dad to take over on the mountain. That gives you some idea how scary it is."

"Oh, I'm so excited! It's the first time I've been to the mountains since summer camp at elementary school. My family never goes on holiday, so other than school trips I reckon this must be the first time I've ever been away from home."

I was feeling a bit gloomy, but seeing how excited my husband was, I was beginning to be glad that we'd come.

"Natsuki, thank you," my husband muttered as he gazed out of the window. "I really was thinking about dying. I'm so glad I could get away from the Factory with you like this before that."

He leaned against me. Maybe he was feeling sleepy. We never touched, so this was highly unusual.

I looked out of the window, feeling the weight of my husband's head on my shoulder. We passed through a few tunnels, signs that we were getting close to the mountains.

Uncle Teruyoshi was waiting at the ticket gate when we arrived at Nagano Station.

"Thank you for going to the trouble of coming out to meet us," I said.

His hair was now completely white, and for a moment I didn't recognize him. The figure waving to me and calling out "Natsuki!" looked more like my grandfather than the uncle I'd known twenty-three years before.

"I've heard all about Akishina from Natsuki. Being able to actually go there is like a dream come true! Thank you so much."

"Oh, the pleasure is all mine. These days it's what you call a critically depopulated village, with lots of empty houses. It's a bit bleak, really. Grandpa will be happy that you youngsters have come all this way to pay him a visit."

Uncle Teruyoshi looked smaller than I remembered. I'd probably also grown a bit since elementary school, but I didn't think that was the only reason.

"Shall we go and have lunch somewhere? Once we get to Akishina, there's no stores or eateries or anything, so it's best to do some shopping for food before we go.

"Thank you, but we already brought pretty much everything we need with us," I said, showing him the big bag I was carrying over my shoulder.

"You haven't changed at all, Natsuki. You always were well prepared," he said with a smile.

"Do you mind if I go to the bathroom before we set off?" my husband asked.

As he ran off to find the bathroom, Uncle Teruyoshi said, "It's quite a bit cooler here than in Tokyo, isn't it? You can wait inside the car if you like."

"No, I'm fine. I also anticipated that and brought a coat with me."

"You did? I guess you know the Akishina weather well, too, Natsuki," he said, the corners of his eyes crinkling. "I told Yuu that you were coming. He himself said it would be better if he stayed somewhere else, but it's not easy at such short notice."

"I'm sorry to have caused such a fuss."

"No, it's fine. That house had been lying empty ever since Granny died and was a bit desolate. There had been talk of demolishing it since it's so run-down, so I was happy when Yuu said he wanted to stay there. It somehow felt a bit like the old days. The two of you always did love that house, didn't you?" Uncle murmured, narrowing his eyes as he reeled in the memories. Then he looked down. "I felt really bad about what happened back then, you know."

I looked at him in surprise.

"You were both just children and didn't know any better. And all of us adults totally overreacted. We tried to put a lid on it to cover it up. Adults are so violent and overbearing, they really are."

"Not at all . . . well now that I've grown up I can understand the circumstances better. You didn't do anything wrong, Uncle Teruyoshi."

"Does your husband know about what happened? Sorry if I'm sticking my nose in where it's not wanted."

"You don't need to worry about him," I said flatly.

He looked a little relieved and smiled. "You married well, didn't you?"

"Are you okay? You don't look too good," I said to my husband.

"I'll be okay," he groaned, holding a handkerchief over his mouth.

Uncle Teruyoshi drove skillfully around the hairpin bends. The mountain road was steeper and narrower than I remembered, with a cliff dropping off to one side, and there weren't any guard rails. Every time we went around a curve, our bottoms slid over the back seat and squashed our bodies against each other.

"It's tough for people who aren't used to it. Shall I stop somewhere for a rest?"

"No, I'm okay."

"Really? If you can cope, then it's definitely better to get it over and done with. These bends are really hard to deal with when you don't know them. Are you doing okay, Natsuki?"

"Yes, I'm fine," I said bravely, although actually I was feeling quite uneasy about falling off the edge. I didn't want Uncle to think I'd gone soft living in the metropolis and had forgotten how wild the Akishina mountains were.

"You haven't changed at all, have you, Natsuki?" Uncle said, looking pleased.

The tension of meeting after such a long time was beginning to dissipate, and I could feel the beloved uncle who had always spoiled me as a kid coming through.

"Just three more bends to go, and we'll be there. Hold on just a bit longer!"

Leaves scratched against the window. I had the feeling that the greenery was pressing in on us with a greater intensity than it had long ago. I was up against the window gazing at the trees like I'd done as a child. We climbed up and up the unfamiliar winding tunnel of green until my ears started popping painfully, then suddenly the vista opened out before us.

"We're here! Natsuki and Tomoya, welcome to Akishina!" he announced, bringing tears to my eyes.

And there, just beyond the familiar small red bridge, was the Akishina that I had replayed in my mind time and time again over the years.

Uncle stopped the car by the red bridge for my husband, who was super excited, his carsickness forgotten.

"Uncle, is this the same river where we used to light the fire for the ancestors back when we were kids?"

I couldn't resist getting out of the car and running to the river, which now seemed more like a tiny shallow stream.

"Yes, that's right. Don't you remember?"

"I thought it was wider and deeper . . . I remember when we were little we'd sometimes put on our bathing suits and go swimming."

"You did? This river is far too shallow for swimming, though. When I was a kid I remember me and my friends built a dam with stones to make a pool to swim in. I guess we must have done the same when you and the others were coming so everyone could enjoy playing in the water."

"Oh."

Come to think of it, the river had been dammed with stones. I'd tried so hard to keep Akishina vivid in my mind, but my memories of the place had become patchy.

The mountains surrounding the village were much higher than I remembered. My image of them was green, but here and there the leaves had started to take on a red autumnal tinge. In my memory, my grandfather's grave was some distance away, but I could see it now, just the other side of the river.

"The utility poles aren't made of wood anymore."

"That's right. Long ago they did used to be wood, didn't they? You have got a good memory! You still can't get cell phone reception here, but since that's going to be a big problem when the grandkids start coming here, there is talk of putting up an antenna."

"Really? You'll be able to use smartphones in Akishina?"

Akishina had always been there in my thoughts, and now I walked unsteadily along the road by the river, feeling that the reality didn't quite fit with the image in my mind, as if I'd suddenly experienced a twenty-three-year time slip. Some things were as I remembered, but other things were different. It felt strange, as though I'd entered a parallel world.

"Look over there. Do you remember that?"

Uncle was pointing at the dear old storehouse with its thick, white-painted mud walls and red roof. It was completely unchanged.

"Yes! It's exactly as I remembered it!" I broke into a run.

"Is it? I suppose it was a popular hiding place for you kids when playing hide-and-seek, wasn't it?" Uncle called after me with a smile.

"Wow, it's amazing! Oh, wow!" my husband whooped as he caught up with us. He took out his cell phone and started taking pictures.

As we climbed the narrow path up to the storehouse, the garden and the main house came into view. The garden was much smaller than I remembered. The house beyond it looked big even now—with its familiar white plaster walls, dark wooden beams, and steep roof with deep eaves—but since it had lain empty for quite a long period the roof and pillars were a bit run-down.

Uncle knocked on the glass pane of the front door. Maybe there wasn't a doorbell.

"Hello? Yuu, we're here!"

No answer. The interior of the house was silent.

"That's odd. I called him yesterday to let him know we'd be getting here around lunchtime."

Uncle Teruyoshi said he'd go check the back door and climbed up the weed-covered slope next to the house.

My husband and I were left standing at the front. Maybe Yuu had run away, not wanting to meet me. I felt somehow betrayed.

"That bug . . ." my husband murmured.

Some sort of green insect I'd never seen before was about to squeeze through a slight gap in the door into the house. I went to brush it away with my hand when the door suddenly slid open. Disturbed by the sudden movement, the bug flew away.

"Hello? Is anyone home?" I called out nervously and went inside.

The dark, old-fashioned entrance hall was about the size of an entire studio apartment in Tokyo. Inside were some farming tools, a bamboo hat, a hosepipe, some plastic kerosene cans, and rubber boots. In among the dusty rubber boots was a pair of brand-new indigo-color sneakers. It had just occurred to me that these were probably Yuu's, which meant that he must be inside, when the staircase creaked.

"Hello," came a feeble voice, and Yuu appeared.

Twenty-three years had passed since I'd last met him, but he hadn't changed at all. His arms and legs had grown, but his hairstyle was the same, and his facial features hadn't altered much. Superimposing his appearance now onto the Yuu in my memory felt rather strange.

"I'm your cousin Natsuki Sasamoto," I politely introduced myself, thinking that I had perhaps changed quite a lot.

Yuu gave a little smile and murmured quietly, "Natsuki, is it you?"

"And I'm her husband," my husband said awkwardly, bowing his head.

"Uncle Teruyoshi just went around to the back door."

"Oh, sorry! That door's locked. I'll go open it for him."

"Uncle Teruyoshi said he'd phoned you yesterday."

Yuu was wearing a neat white shirt, and I thought uneasily that he looked as though he was on his way out somewhere.

"Yes, I spoke with him. So, you two are going to be staying here for a while, right?"

"I hope we won't be a bother to you."

"Of course not! And anyway, this isn't my house, so please make yourselves at home," he said with a smile and slid open the door through to the living room where we'd often played as children. "Please do come in. I'll just go check the back door. Come in and make yourselves comfortable. It's a bit of a mess I'm afraid. And it is a bit weird for me to be welcoming you in when it's not even my house!"

He put some slippers out for me and my husband, then went down the hall toward the bathroom. As a child, I hadn't known that there'd been another entrance back there.

My husband and I nervously went into the house clutching our bags. I was relieved that Yuu was connecting to me naturally, as if that affair had never happened between the two of us.

"There's a kind of animal smell in here," my husband murmured. I didn't know whether he meant that one had gotten into the house or that the house smelled of humans.

"Oh man, this is so amazing!"

In the living room was the kotatsu, some shelves with my grandmother's stuff on them, and a TV. In my memory, the TV was an old-fashioned one with a dial, but the one there now was the latest flat-screen model.

"Wow, this room is just how I imagined it! Is the veranda over here?" my husband said excitedly as my uncle and Yuu came in.

"You must be tired after traveling for so long. Would you like some tea?"

"Thank you."

"Well, I must get going now," Uncle said. "My grandson is visiting. I promised I'd be back in time for dinner."

My husband and I hastily bowed to him. "So sorry to bring you all the way out here when you're so busy!"

"Oh, no problem! I'm happy to see a bit of life in this house!" My uncle's wrinkled face broke into a smile as he put down his shoes in the entrance hall, hopped into them, and waved goodbye.

When the sound of his car had faded into the distance, the house suddenly felt unnaturally quiet. Feeling a little awkward, I said casually to Yuu, "I can't believe how small this room is! I thought all us cousins used to gather in here at night and play cards!"

Yuu's expression relaxed. "When I came back here, I also thought it was smaller than I remembered."

The three of us sat down at the kotatsu and ate the sweet bean jelly that Yuu had put out, together with green tea. "Try this Nagano delicacy too," Yuu said to Tomoya, fetching some seaweed jelly from the kitchen. He then went on to briefly explain the house setup.

"I'll show you around later, but the bathroom and toilet are down that corridor. The kitchen is through there. We use well water here. It's clean and tastes good, but if you're worried about it I can buy you some mineral water when I go down the mountain. There's only one bus a day, so I'll do the shopping by car. Tell me whenever you need something, and I'll go get it for you."

"What about shopping online?" my husband asked.

"I don't think any stores will deliver here. I don't know if any of the houses up here are even connected to the internet. There isn't a mobile grocery store either. Even most taxis will refuse to bring you out this far, unless the driver knows the road to Akishina. The number for the local taxi service is written down here, but if you ever want to go anywhere just tell me, and I'll drive you," Yuu said. "The house is out of

range for cell phones, but there's a spot just the other side of
the red bridge where you can get reception, so if you want to
send email or whatever, try walking down there. Otherwise,
use the landline for calls. The number's written down here."

"Okay."

"As I said, there aren't any stores here in the village. Or
even vending machines. Even the nearest convenience store
is a good drive away. There's a roadside station, which is good
for buying vegetables, and I go to the local supermarket for
other necessities. Uncle left us some vegetables and rice in the
doma next to the kitchen, so help yourself to those. There are
still quite a few pears left I think."

"Sorry, but what's a doma?" my husband ventured.

"It's like a room with a bare earth floor. Go have a look
at it, and you'll see what I mean."

"Can I see the attic too?" my husband asked, abruptly
leaning forward.

"Sure. You're really into these country houses, aren't you?"
Yuu said with a smile. "As for the toilet, you remember what it
was like when we were kids, Natsuki? It's what we call a drop
toilet, which gives you the general idea. It hasn't changed, so
take care when you use it, okay? The old gas-heated bath is
just the same too."

"Where should we sleep?"

"Wherever you like." Yuu began pointing at various sliding doors around the room. "The upper tatami room is there,
the lower one there, the altar room there. Take a look around

the house and decide which room you want to use. I'm currently in the room at the top of the stairs, so you can choose anywhere other than that."

My husband started to get up. "Is that the silkworm room?!"

"No, what used to be the silkworm room is the one next to it at the far end, I think . . . You really do know a lot about this place, don't you? Has Natsuki been telling you stories?"

Taken aback at being addressed, I nodded.

"I see. Funny that you remembered the silkworms. Anyway, you can use anywhere except the room right by the top of the stairs. Although since you are a couple, I would have thought one of the bigger rooms would be best."

"Well, actually we'd like to sleep in separate rooms if you don't mind," my husband said apologetically. "We're a bit different from your usual couple. We're married, but we're not so close that we actually sleep together."

"Huh?" Yuu said, tilting his head questioningly.

"I don't mind sleeping with other people in the same room, but Tomoya doesn't like it. We always get single rooms when traveling together too. If you're not using the room where Granny used to sleep, then I'd be grateful if he could sleep there. I don't mind where I sleep. I can sleep in the silkworm room or the altar room, whichever.

"Um, well . . ."

Seeing Yuu look so disconcerted, my husband and I exchanged a glance.

"Seeing as we're going to be staying here a while, maybe we should tell him the truth about us?" he asked.

"Yeah, I guess," I said, nodding.

Yuu gaped at us, an uneasy look on his face.

I started telling Yuu the story. "Do you remember Planet Popinpobopia?"

As a child I'd disliked seaweed jelly, but now I was enjoying its refreshing texture. Next to me, my husband was eating it with relish.

"Er, yes, I remember," Yuu nodded after a moment's silence and glanced at my husband.

"Not long after that happened, I found out that actually I was from that planet too. Piyyut told me, and I told Tomoya about it. But now there's no hope of a spaceship coming, right? So all I can do is keep my head down and pretend to live as an Earthling. I thought that when I grew up society would brainwash me, but it didn't work. I'm tired, so I decided to come and rest here for a while. The stars are closer here too."

Yuu glanced at my husband again. "I see. I had no idea."

"I don't particularly love my wife, but I married her in order to divert the attention of the Factory. Unlike her, I'm terrified of being brainwashed. The Factory really is frightening, you know. It makes us into slaves."

"Sorry, but what is this Factory you're talking about?" Yuu asked him, choosing his words carefully.

"Oh, that's what we call the society we live in. After all, that's what it is, right? We are physically connected components. Parts that just keep on manufacturing children, carrying our genes forward into the future. I'd always been kind of creeped out by it ever since I was a kid, but when I met Natsuki I was finally able to see it for what it was," my husband said. "You see, that's when the alien eye was downloaded into me too," he added, touching his eyelid.

"The alien eye?"

Yuu looked puzzled, so I explained it to him as clearly as I could. "He means the way aliens see human society. Probably everyone has it. They just don't normally realize."

"That's right. It was always inside me too," my husband said. "Now it seems the alien eye is stronger in me than in Natsuki."

Yuu seemed somewhat bemused at our vigorous assertions. "I, er . . . I see. You two do seem to have well-matched values, don't you?"

"No, what we call values are also part of the Factory's brainwashing! Natsuki wants to be brainwashed by the Factory, so that someday she'll be able to live as an Earthling rather than a Popinpobopian, but not me. I personally think the alien eye is important."

My husband was leaning forward as he talked, and Yuu glanced at me as if asking for help.

"Tomoya, calm down. You're scaring him!"

My husband snapped back into himself and sat back in his seat apologetically. "I'm sorry, I try to stop myself from talking about this. I am always keeping my head down so as not to be exposed by the Factory."

Unlike me, my husband really hated the Factory. As far as I was concerned, though, I would never be able to return to my home planet without a spaceship, so the sooner I was brainwashed the better.

"Have you never thought like that yourself, Yuu? Society is a factory, and you're an alien, that sort of thing?" my husband asked.

Yuu smiled. "No, never. I might have had that kind of fantasy when I was little, but I'm an adult now. I'm a fully fledged Earthling, and I'll live out my life on this planet."

Night fell, and Yuu wanted to go down the mountain to get some more local Nagano delicacies for us, but we didn't want to put him to that sort of trouble. In the end, we decided to make a simple hotpot from whatever we could find in the fridge and doma.

My husband chopped up vegetables, and Yuu served up rice from the rice cooker. I found and washed some tableware for us to use.

"This really takes me back," I said when I saw the glasses with blue and red flowers on them.

When we were little, we cousins would always fight over who got to use them. I liked the glass with the blue flower best, because it struck me as more grown-up, but Yota also thought it was cool and would refuse point-blank to give it up.

"Really? You mean we used to use these glasses when we were little too?"

"Yes! Yota and I would always fight over this one, and I sometimes even made him cry! Don't you remember?"

"No, I don't remember that. Yota lives in Ueda now, and he sometimes comes to see me here, you know. He had a little girl recently, so he'll probably bring her, too, when she's a little bigger."

"Wouldn't it be great if all the cousins' kids could gather here and play together, just like we used to back then?"

"Yes, wouldn't it! Maybe someday."

My husband didn't join our conversation as he carried the chopped vegetables through to the living room to cook on the tabletop gas burner. He didn't much like talk about children and relatives. He was instinctively averse to the suggestion that blood connections and family gatherings were enjoyable. For him they were all part of the brainwashing by the Factory. He was probably right to some extent, but I was also curious to see what the children who had inherited my grandfather's genes looked like. I was probably more brainwashed than my husband and a bit closer to being an Earthling.

"Natsuki, it's really like you've been frozen in time, isn't it?"

"Is it?"

"You remember all of it, every detail about this place."

"I guess so."

There were things that didn't match my memory, and I found that disorientating, but it probably didn't seem that way to Yuu. He put the bowls of rice on a tray and went through to the living room. Left alone in the kitchen, I turned on the faucet to wash the glasses, and the cold water from the mountain spring splashed off the back of my hand and spattered my blouse.

Once we'd finished our simple meal, we each went to our separate rooms to sleep.

After some discussion, it was decided that Yuu would continue to use the room at the top of the stairs, while my husband would sleep in the silkworm room. My husband was super excited by this, saying it was like a dream come true.

I decided to sleep in the altar room. I liked the aroma of incense, and I wouldn't be able to relax in the other bigger rooms farther in.

I brought down some bedding from upstairs and laid it out on the tatami floor. The feel of my head lying on the pillow filled with buckwheat chaff took me back.

Come to think of it, it had been a long time since I had last slept in a wooden house. The ceiling creaked faintly, and the sliding doors rattled, communicating the presence of two other animals other than myself in the house.

As I closed my eyes, the chirring of insects outside pressed against the windows. Not the summer insects, this was the sound of autumn. Before I knew it, I'd fallen asleep to the noise of the creaking floorboards upstairs.

CHAPTER 4

Being back in Akishina, all kinds of childhood memories began resurfacing. Like, for example, how I killed the Wicked Witch at Mr. Igasaki's place.

I don't really remember much about what happened after that incident with Yuu; it all seems like a dream now. As soon as we arrived back home from Nagano, I was shut up in my bedroom. A large padlock was placed on the outside of the door, and when nobody else was home it was locked. If I wanted to go to the toilet, I had to wait until my sister or Mom came home.

Whenever I phoned my friends, either my sister or Mom would keep watch over me to make sure I wasn't talking to Yuu. For the rest of the summer holiday, I spent pretty much all my time locked up in my room.

I passed the days in the gloom staring at our marriage pledge and my ring. Gradually something strange happened. I began to see my transformation mirror and origami wand become filled with particles of light. I could hear Piyyut's voice clearly talking to me. He would often talk to me now that he'd been freed from the spell cast by the evil forces.

When I asked Piyyut if my magical powers were growing stronger, his answer came back crystal clear, "Yes, that's right!"

All the same, my mouth was still broken. I couldn't taste food, and eating wasn't at all enjoyable. When I was called downstairs for meals, I would hardly eat a thing before going back to my room. Mom would say with a sigh that I was being "rebellious."

One day I had just taken a single bite of a tasteless hamburger and was about to go back to my room when Mom told me, "You'll be doing the intensive course at cram school again this year, you know." It was just over a month since Grandpa had died.

"Why? I thought I wasn't supposed to leave my room."

"For heaven's sake, stop quibbling! You're going, and that's that. And if you're even slightly late home, I'll inform the police. You got that?"

I'd lost all sense of the passing of days, and when I went back to my room I looked at the calendar. My countdown to Obon was still recorded there: Three days to go . . . Two days to go . . . The day we'd gone to Akishina was marked THE END in small letters. After that I hadn't made any entries. The calendar was completely blank. I recalled how I really had intended to end it all that day.

I searched in my bag and found the printout from cram school. The intensive course was due to start in three days' time. The night before, Mr. Igasaki phoned and Mom answered so loudly that I could hear her from my room upstairs.

"Oh, Mr. Igasaki! Thank you so much for taking the trouble to call! You tried calling before? Well, you see, we had some unfortunate news and had to return to my husband's family home. Yes, of course. After all, she was lucky enough to participate in your intensive course last year too. She absolutely loves your classes, Mr. Igasaki. Yes, yes of course, I'll tell her."

Mom practically forced me to take the receiver. I held it to my right ear. "I'm here waiting for you," Mr. Igasaki said cheerfully. His breath passed through the receiver and stuck fast to my ear. I couldn't move.

From that day, it wasn't just my mouth that was broken but my right ear too. It wasn't completely broken like my mouth was, but sometimes I couldn't hear what was happening right in front of me and instead heard a sound like waves or a continuous buzzing. Meanwhile Piyyut's voice grew steadily clearer.

I devoted myself to practicing my magic. I was particularly assiduous about practicing the out-of-body experience. If I could just perfect this, maybe I could go somewhere far away. Yet I never could really manage it.

Survive, whatever it takes.

These words were all I was left with. The only way I could survive was through my magical powers.

The first day of the intensive course, my sister came along to keep watch, following me on her bicycle as I made my way to the cram school.

"If you try to run away, I'll beat you with this," she told me, showing me a short bamboo sword she kept in her tote bag, the sort of thing sold in souvenir shops.

Soon, though, she relaxed her vigilance since her own summer course was starting. Mr. Igasaki wasted no time in taking advantage of this and asked me, "Natsuki, do you have some free time tomorrow?"

"Yes." My right ear filled with the sound of waves and Piyyut's voice.

"Tomorrow there isn't any cram school, so I'll give you a special lesson. I showed you where the key to my house is kept, didn't I? How about midday? Come to my house again at that time. You understand, don't you? This is a special lesson, so you mustn't tell anyone else. And tell your mother that you are coming to the usual intensive course, all right?"

"Yes."

That night I consulted with Piyyut.

"Your teacher is a pawn for the evil forces," he told me. "He's operated by the Wicked Witch, so you have to save him."

The Wicked Witch had already broken my mouth and my right ear. If I didn't quickly use my magical powers to transform and defeat her, next time she would probably kill me.

Survive, whatever it takes.

Piyyut whispered this to me over and over, as if he was channeling Yuu.

Tomorrow the Wicked Witch possessing Mr. Igasaki might completely destroy my body. I only had tonight to act if I was going to defeat her and survive. I put Piyyut and my transformation mirror into my backpack, along with my magic wand, and slipped out of the house.

It seemed my parents and sister had let their guard down, perhaps because I'd been completely docile ever since they'd started keeping watch over me. It was surprisingly easy to escape.

I silently opened the door and went outside. Suddenly, a thought occurred to me. Taking care not to make any sound, I opened the garden shed to look for something that might aid me in the fight against the Witch. "Ouch!" Something sharp pricked my finger as I fumbled in the dark. I put on some gloves that were lying on the floor and rummaged around on the shelves.

I armed myself with several items, and just as I was closing up the shed I came across a flashlight, so I put that in my backpack too.

I headed for the house that Mr. Igasaki had taken me to after the summer festival.

Piyyut was especially talkative, chattering away in my right ear.

Hurry. Hurry! If the Wicked Witch kills you, it'll bring about the end of the world. Only your magical powers can prevent that.

You've got to give it your best! You've got to do what it takes to survive.

As I ran to Mr. Igasaki's house I looked at my Snoopy watch: three o'clock. I was used to three o'clock being the time for my afternoon snack, and it was weird to think there was another three o'clock in the middle of the night.

Unlike in Akishina, night in the Factory was ablaze with a multitude of street lamps, and few stars were visible in the sky. Lights were on in some houses despite the late hour. This was the Baby Factory, after all, so new babies were probably being manufactured throughout the night. I suddenly felt sick as I ran, and I vomited the gastric juice that welled up into my mouth into a flowerbed.

When I arrived at Mr. Igasaki's house, I took the front-door key from under the third plant pot from the right, just as he'd shown me. He had told me that whenever he phoned, I should take that key and let myself into the house. I wondered whether the Wicked Witch knew that Mr. Igasaki had shown me where the key was.

Even though I had the key, I was scared of going inside, and for a while I tried to use my out-of-body spell. I couldn't get it to work, though, and instead Piyyut's voice in my right ear grew steadily louder.

Hurry! Hurry! Hurry! If you dawdle like this, the Wicked Witch will be able to prepare some frightening magic. You have to destroy her before she kills you. You're a warrior for justice, you know. If you die, it'll mean the end of the world. Hurry! Hurry! Hurry!

I had to save the world. I obeyed Piyyut and crept into Mr. Igasaki's house.

Inside everything was in silence, and the air was absolutely still. Maybe Mr. Igasaki wasn't at home tonight. I would peek into his room, and if neither he nor the Wicked Witch were there, then I would go home for the night.

I kept telling myself that they definitely weren't here so it was okay, and suddenly I felt strangely brave. Just in case, I took out a weapon from my backpack and headed for the stairs.

I felt weak, like I had that day. Just as I thought I wouldn't be able to take a single step farther, the electronic buzzing inside my right ear grew louder, and I crouched down.

. . . ki, Natsuki, Natsuki!

Hearing Piyyut's voice, I looked up and saw that the interior of Mr. Igasaki's house, the walls, the ceilings, had all turned pink. Surprised, I looked at my hands and saw they were pink too. It was as though I'd walked into a single-color photo printed in pink.

Natsuki, the world has turned pink due to the strength of your magical powers! Now you'll definitely be able to beat the Wicked Witch. Hurry hurry hurry!

Piyyut's voice was so loud I thought it must be ringing out throughout the house. It was so loud it was splitting my skull. Clutching my head, I started to climb the pink staircase.

Maybe the Witch had broken my eyes too. The thought scared me. My mouth, my right ear, my eyes . . . what would she break next?

I stood before the door to Mr. Igasaki's room.

The thought briefly crossed my mind that I should run away. What on earth had possessed me to come here? A little girl with half-baked magical powers unable even to use her out-of-body spell was hardly likely to defeat the Wicked Witch.

No sound came from the room.

Just then, I felt as though something big was approaching.

It was the out-of-body power. Before I knew what was happening, I had left my body the way I had the day of the summer festival and was watching myself.

You did it! You summoned the power!

I'd succeeded at last, but I only felt numb. My body opened the door and silently went inside. The out-of-body me watched intently as it did so.

Mr. Igasaki was asleep on the bed. For some reason, I no longer felt any fear. My body slowly approached his sleeping form.

The next moment, my vision crumpled, and the sensation of smashing something soft came through my palms.

Before me was a blue lump, and I was raining down blows on that lump with the small grass-cutting scythe Dad had brought from Akishina, the one I had taken from the shed.

The out-of-body power ended all of a sudden. A golden liquid was spurting from the blue lump. What was this? It must be the pupa of the Wicked Witch, my intuition told me. I had to kill her before she hatched. I knew that if I didn't, something terrible would happen.

Mr. Igasaki was nowhere in the room, so he must have already been eaten by the Witch. The golden liquid was spraying all over the room.

Now's your chance! Say the magic word! Cast the spell!

I had never practiced magic words with Piyyut. I said the first word that came in to my head, over and over again.

"Popinpobopia, Popinpobopia, Popinpobopia, Popinpobopia, Popinpobopia."

I had no idea whether this counted as a spell. Golden liquid was steadily spurting from the blue lump.

Hurryhurryhurry! Killkillkill! WitchWitchWitchWitch! Killkillkillkill!

"PopinpobopiaPopinpobopiaPopinpobopiaPopinpobopiaPopinpobopiaPopinpobopiaPopinpobopiaPopinpobopiaPopinpobopiaPopinpobopia."

I desperately kept repeating the magic word as Piyyut told me to, while sticking the scythe into the bright blue lump over and over again.

I don't know how long I carried on doing this. I have the feeling it was just one minute, but it could have been several hours.

That's enough! That's not enough! That's enough! That's not enough! Piyyut sang.

"PopinpobopiaPopinpobopiaPopinpobopiaPopinpobo-
piaPopinpobopiaPopinpobopiaPopinpobopiaPopinpobopi-
aPopinpobopiaPopinpobopia."

By the time Piyyut stopped singing "That's not enough!" and just sang "That's enough!" the blue lump was no longer moving.

The magic would probably soon wear off. I noticed that the origami wand I'd shoved into my pocket was all crumpled and no longer gave out any particles of light. The spell was broken. I hurried out of Mr. Igasaki's house.

"My clothes are dirty," I muttered to Piyyut. My clothes were soaked with the golden liquid that had spurted from the blue lump.

I suddenly remembered that Mr. Igasaki's house was close to my elementary school. I ran there and took off all my clothes and, lighting my way with the flashlight, put them into the incinerator in the school yard. I threw the gloves and the scythe in too. My backpack wasn't too dirty, so I hoisted it onto my back and hurried back home in my underwear.

I went in through the door quietly, then, realizing my hands were sticky, I hurried to the bathroom and, still wearing my backpack, took a shower.

That's enough! That's enough! That's not enough! That's not enough!

I was still hearing Piyyut singing loudly in my right ear.

"What are you doing in there?" my sister's voice came from outside the bathroom door.

I jumped. My pink vision suddenly returned to normal, and my own emaciated flesh-colored features appeared in the bathroom mirror.

"Nothing. I sweated a lot yesterday, and I suddenly felt like having a shower."

"I suppose you wet your bed? You're still a baby, after all." My sister laughed then went away, apparently satisfied.

I wrapped my sodden backpack in a towel and, hugging it to me, went back to my room.

My body felt heavy and I was terribly sleepy, exhausted from using all my magical powers.

That's not enough! That's not enough! That's enough! That's enough!

Piyyut's song looped endlessly in my ear. Somehow I felt extremely relaxed. I quickly fell fast asleep.

The next day, I had a fever and stayed in bed. My temperature went up to nearly forty degrees, and I was taken to hospital in case it was influenza. I was diagnosed with a cold and exhaustion.

"And she hasn't been eating properly, has she? Her immune system is weak, you know," the doctor said.

For some reason Mom answered, "I'm sorry," and bowed deeply.

My fever still didn't subside, and I stayed in bed until the start of the new semester.

It was only when my fever finally let up and I went back to school and saw Shizuka that I heard Mr. Igasaki had been murdered.

"Didn't you know? Mr. Igasaki was murdered by some pervert."

"I didn't know . . ."

Shizuka looked as though she'd been crying. Her eyes were all red, and she was clutching a handkerchief.

"Mr. Igasaki was so amazingly cool! That's why he was targeted by a pervert. He'd been bothered by a stalker. He'd told a friend of his at university about it. They said he was so scared he couldn't sleep at night and was taking sleeping pills. So when the pervert finally got into the house, he didn't realize and was murdered in his sleep. It's just awful!"

"Oh, it really is! Awful!" I shouted, imitating Shizuka's tone of voice.

"They haven't found any witnesses at all, apparently. Mr. Igasaki's family are handing out flyers at the station calling for people to come forward. All of us at the cram school loved Mr. Igasaki, didn't we? So we wrote a letter to his parents, saying that we must try to find the murderer and would help handing out the flyers. You'll join us too, won't you, Natsuki?"

"Of course!"

When I got home, I pulled out the newspaper from a few days earlier and found a report headed: ONE LESS SMILING FACE—ROBBED OF A YOUNG LIFE OVERNIGHT. According to this paper, the handsome young university student was being stalked and had been so stressed out he'd been prescribed sleeping tablets. He was such a kind young man that he couldn't even talk to his parents about it and had only confessed his worries to a close friend. Mr. Igasaki was working part-time as a teacher in a cram school and was adored by all the children. The murder happened during the summer while his parents were away on business, and he was stabbed multiple times. His wounds were so terrible that they had to identify him from his dental records. The murderer had not yet been found, but Mr. Igasaki had told his friend that he was being followed by a white van, and the police were seeking witnesses with information on any suspect vans in the area.

It was a strange feeling. So what was the blue lump I'd killed? Mr. Igasaki hadn't even been there. I'd only done battle with the Wicked Witch, but the Witch herself had disappeared without a trace.

The hearing in my right ear still came and went. My mouth was completely broken, I could only sense if something was hot or cold. I still had no appetite, but Mom was strict about not wasting any food so I forced myself to finish meals at home, although at school I got away with eating less.

Every Saturday and Sunday after cram school I went to the station and joined Mr. Igasaki's family in handing out flyers. They read: "Appeal for witnesses! The murderer who robbed us of a precious life mustn't get away with it!"

Mr. Igasaki's parents were an extremely well-mannered, refined couple, and I firmly returned their handshake as they tearfully thanked each of us in turn.

Every day when I went home, I would try talking with Piyyut.

You killed the Wicked Witch. You killed the Wicked Witch. Thank you! Thank you!

Whatever I asked him, that's all he would say.

"Where did that blue lump go? Maybe Mr. Igasaki was killed by the Wicked Witch rather than by a pervert?"

You killed the Wicked Witch! Thank you! Thank you!

He just kept repeating the same phrases over and over again, as if he was broken.

Had the Wicked Witch that day been a dream? I was beginning to wonder whether that was actually the case.

I carried on handing out flyers outside the station with friends from cram school. One day we were on our way home when Shizuka told me, "It seems they haven't found the murder weapon. The police suspect it's not a knife but something like a garden scythe."

"A garden scythe?"

"What was that pervert thinking. It's so scary! I hope they arrest him soon."

"So scary!" I said, imitating Shizuka, thinking to myself that the murderer must have found the scythe I used to kill the Wicked Witch and used it to murder Mr. Igasaki.

First thing on Monday morning I rushed to the school incinerator, but I couldn't find any trace of the items I'd thrown away that day. I thought that at least the blade if not the clothes must be left, but all that was in there was photocopy paper and regular trash.

I went back home and looked at the backpack that I'd stuffed under the bed back when it was still wet, expecting to see some of the gold liquid stuck to it, but instead there were only some small black stains on the shoulder straps.

Every night I tried to talk to Piyyut.

"Piyyut, I think the murderer may have stolen the weapon I killed the Wicked Witch with."

Natsuki, thank you! Natsuki, thank you!

"Hey Piyyut, answer me, will you? I'm worried. I mean . . . what if . . . what if Mr. Igasaki . . ."

Noticing my serious tone, after a short pause, Piyyut said in my right ear, even louder than usual: *Natsuki, let me give you some good news. Thanks to you, the Wicked Witch's magic has completely disappeared from the world. So now there's no more need for you to transform yourself or fight. Soon you won't be able to hear my voice anymore.*

"Why?"

Because our mission here is over. I have one last thing to tell you. I found you, gave you the mirror and the wand and your magical powers. But that wasn't by chance. You were a magic warrior sent from Planet Popinpobopia when you were a baby.

Actually, once your mission was over, you were supposed to return to Planet Popinpobopia. But it took longer than expected, and the spaceship isn't around anymore.

"I see. So I'm not an Earthling, after all! I was a Popinpobopian all along!"

I was so excited I clung tight to Piyyut. Piyyut looked pleased and wiggled his ears.

That's right! You'd already begun to suspect that was the case, hadn't you? You'd begun to think that maybe, just maybe, you weren't an Earthling. That's why you didn't really fit in, and of course you thought Earthlings were strange. After all, you're a Popinpobopian.

"Yay! I'm so happy! So that's what it was!"

"All we Popinpobopians are singing your praises, you know. Everyone is overjoyed."

"Will I be able to go home someday?"

Piyyut said something, but I didn't hear what it was.

I fell into a deep sleep. The backpack I'd hidden under the bed was dirty. Tomorrow I would throw it away. And I wouldn't be using the mirror and wand inside it anymore either. But it was enough just to have been told that I was a Popinpobopian. As I slept, I found myself back under the starry sky at Akishina for the first time in a long while.

After that night, Piyyut never spoke another word again. It was as though he'd been mummified. I laid him carefully to rest in the tin box along with my other important items, the marriage pledge with Yuu and my wedding ring.

The investigation into Mr. Igasaki's murder stalled. Now and then his family and some cram school pupils would be shown on the local TV channel handing out flyers. I was there with them, encouraged by Shizuka.

Everyone gossiped about how terribly sad it was that such a lovely young university student had been murdered by a pervert, but deep down they somehow seemed strangely glad about it.

From that point on, I lost my magical powers and thereafter lived as an ordinary Popinpobopian, adrift from her spaceship and unable to go home. Life as a Popinpobopian was lonely. I just hoped the Earthlings would succeed in brainwashing me.

CHAPTER 5

When I woke the next morning, my husband was already up and about in the garden.

"Can I have a look inside the storehouse? I'd better wait until Yuu gets up, of course."

"Sure, but I doubt you'll find anything much of interest. I used to love exploring it when I was little, but I only ever saw farming stuff in there."

"I don't mind, I just want to see inside it!"

My husband had been such a recluse in Tokyo, but here he was so cheerful and energetic. I had the feeling that I was looking at my childhood self.

"Good morning! You're up early."

Yuu appeared on the veranda in a sweatshirt and pants.

"Good morning, Tomoya."

"Good morning! Oh, it was my turn to make breakfast this morning, wasn't it?"

My husband hurriedly slipped off his sandals and went back inside.

"I'll help," Yuu said.

"But then there'd be no point in taking turns! Just take it easy and enjoy the morning air. I want to try making miso soup with the wild herbs I picked yesterday."

"Don't make anything too weird, now," I said, a little worried, but he was raring to go.

"It might be a little bitter, but I'm keen to taste it. Oh, how wonderful it is here!" he said, heading off to the kitchen.

"You'd better put something warmer on. Otherwise you'll catch cold," Yuu told me before heading off to the bathroom.

I sat down on the veranda, feeling the old wooden house creaking faintly as Yuu and my husband moved around inside.

Every morning after breakfast the three of us would go for a walk. Yuu had remarked that this was his habit, and my husband said he wanted to go with him.

First we went as far as the red bridge to get reception on our phones to check email and missed calls. Then we would walk slowly along the river until we reached the mountain trail leading to the next village, where we turned around and came back to the house.

Everything seemed novel to my husband. He wanted to go to the next village, but Yuu warned him that the mountain trail was quite tough and he grudgingly gave up the idea.

Sometimes we changed our route and either headed farther up the mountain or down to the abandoned school, but mostly we just wandered along the river.

Now and then we went to make an offering at my grandparents' grave. On those occasions, Yuu always went back alone and never came with us as far as the grave.

Whenever we were walking, I was assailed by a very strange feeling. It was very odd to see my husband and Yuu walking along side by side. Until very recently, Yuu had belonged to my past and my husband to the present, and it felt like one had turned up out of a time machine.

My husband was always super excited and talkative when out walking.

"While I'm here, I want to take the opportunity to do things that humans absolutely don't do."

"Why's that?" Yuu asked.

"Because that will undo my brainwashing," my husband answered confidently. "Taboos are just a form of brainwashing too. Seen through an alien eye none of them are worth bothering about. They are irrational."

"What sort of things do you want to do?"

"I dunno . . . eat something weird, like insects, for example."

"I'm afraid people around here have always eaten bugs. And they eat grasshoppers in various other regions of Japan, don't they, not just in Nagano?"

"Oh, really?"

"If you're interested, I'll buy some for you next time I go shopping. In some places they eat grasshoppers and hornet larvae, oh, and the pupae of those silkworms you love so much, Tomoya. Although my uncle told me that in this house they never ate the silkworm pupae."

"Wow! I definitely want to try those. They're so adorable."

My husband and Yuu had been getting pretty close these past few days. Yuu was making a point of talking with him a lot, while also putting as much distance as he possibly could between himself and me.

"If the town we live in is a Baby Factory," my husband said seriously, "this place is an abandoned factory, isn't it? A factory where nothing gets produced anymore. And where nobody expects to make anything either. I feel so much more comfortable here. I wish I could live the rest of my life here as a discarded, worn-out component."

"I still get hassled here sometimes, too, though. You're young, the villagers say. Go get yourself a wife and have kids."

"That's the ghost of the factory. Abandoned places always have ghosts," my husband said, his face serious.

Amused, Yuu laughed. "Yes, there are probably a whole load of ghosts in this village!"

I could hear the sound of water.

Water still flowed in the river that was so much smaller than it had been in my memory. Even after I had stopped coming to Akishina, its sound had been always there within me.

It was strange to see the real-life Yuu walking alongside the sound of flowing water.

On the other side of the river, I could see the graves of our ancestors. When I was in college, I overheard Uncle Teruyoshi and Dad talking on the phone about how the earth on my grandfather's grave hadn't fallen in yet. Over twenty years had passed since he died, but even now the mound covering his coffin still hadn't fallen in.

What did he look like now under that earth? I had attended a number of funerals of the parents of friends or coworkers, but those had been cremations. His had been the only burial. I wondered if any of his hair or skin was left. I'd looked up how long it took for a body to completely turn to soil and found it was over a hundred years, so maybe he was less changed than I'd imagined and was watching us now.

"Natsuki, is anything wrong?" asked my husband, turning to look back at me still standing in the same spot.

I ran over to join them. I watched as some crows on the other side of the river began to cluster around the food we'd left as offerings on my grandparents' grave.

* * *

Our fall vacation was to be one month. That was our limit.

If we stayed any longer, our savings would run out, and people from the Factory wouldn't keep quiet either. If we were found out, we would be dragged back home.

"You'd better go back before winter, you know," Yuu warned us. "It snows a lot here. Sometimes the first floor gets completely buried."

My husband looked disappointed, but I knew we couldn't expect to have any longer than that.

From the road outside the house, you could see a high mountain. Day by day it was turning redder, and now over half of it was covered in fall colors.

After our morning walk, we would eat grilled oyaki dumplings and discuss what to do that day. Yuu said he would do some gardening, while my husband said he wanted to look for sour dock. I wasn't sure sour dock grew this late in the year, but he was raring to search for some and wasn't about to let that stop him. I still couldn't taste anything, so even if we did find any I wouldn't be able to enjoy its sourness. That made me sad, so I decided to stay in the house and tidy up the tableware.

"These glasses really bring back memories. I wonder if Uncle Teruyoshi would let me take one home with me."

"You'd better check with Aunt Ritsuko. She might want to keep them."

"Okay."

Beyond the veranda, the trees in the garden were also beginning to change color. Gazing at them, I murmured, "It's the first time I've ever seen Akishina in the fall. It was always summer when we came here. I can't imagine what it must look like in the snow."

Keeping his gaze averted from me, Yuu said, "The snow's always deep here in winter."

"I know, just I can't picture it."

"That's because you only see the things visible to you, Natsuki," he said pointedly.

I looked down. "But so does everyone," I argued back in a small voice.

"Plenty of people look squarely at things they don't want to see and live with them."

It had begun to dawn on me since meeting Yuu again and telling him I was an alien that he despised me.

"I bet the snowy landscape is really beautiful, too, different again from the fall colors," my husband said dreamily. "Having spent all my life in Tokyo, I've never seen deep snow. It must be so pretty!"

"It's not as idyllic as all that, you know," Yuu said, his expression softening as he smiled at my husband.

"But the harshness of winter is part and parcel of this village. I'd love to experience it," my husband murmured, although he knew it was most likely impossible.

"This place really has gotten under your skin, hasn't it, Tomoya?"

While Yuu chided my husband, he never contradicted him outright. This was the Yuu that I knew. Even when his own mother had treated him practically as a husband, and even when I'd pushed him to marry me, he had never once refused. Submission had been a coping strategy for him as a child I realized.

"Of course! I want to see for myself what it's like here in winter and spring, but I don't suppose I'll get the chance. You never know what that Factory lot will do," my husband murmured.

We both felt it. It wouldn't be long before an envoy would arrive from the Factory. We were shirking our responsibilities as components and would soon be forced to return. And actually, I was longing for that envoy. We would be taken back to the Factory, where my husband would be put to work, and I would be calmly but coercively encouraged to have a baby. Everyone would lecture me on how wonderful it would be.

I was ready for it. This time everyone would ensure I was perfectly brainwashed, and my body would become a Factory component.

My womb and my husband's testes did not belong to us. The sooner I was brainwashed the better. That way I would no longer suffer. I, too, would be able to live with a smile on my face in the virtual reality world in which everyone was living.

Had my wish come true? The very next day, an envoy arrived at the house in Akishina.

I had just finished lunch and was brushing my teeth in the washroom when I heard a knock on the door.

"Coming!" I called out.

I opened the door to see my sister standing there. She was holding my niece's hand. I felt her briefly grin when she noticed I was still in pajamas.

"Natsuki, do we have a visitor?" Yuu called, peeking out of the kitchen. Seeing my sister there, his face instantly hardened.

"Good morning, Yuu. It's been a long time. I'm Kise. Do you remember me?"

"Er, yes. It has been a long time."

"You two seem to have extended your stay somewhat," she said to me. "Mom's beginning to get worried, so I came to check how things were going." She sounded almost euphoric. The way she was talking was so contrived that I wondered whether she was imitating one of her TV dramas.

"Oh, Kise, how *lovely* to see you!" my husband said loudly, coming out of the living room. He sounded even more theatrical than she did.

My husband hated my sister.

She was one of those who, upon becoming an adult, had achieved salvation in the Factory. As a child, she hadn't been able to properly assimilate into society but had found redemption in becoming a tool of the Factory and had grown into its fervent devotee.

My husband always said disparagingly behind her back, "Even by Factory standards, she really gives me the creeps."

I showed her into the living room and poured her some tea. My niece, who would soon be starting elementary school, was having fun running around the house.

"You're not thinking of staying here forever I suppose?" my sister said to me. She didn't touch the oyaki dumplings that Yuu had put out for her, claiming she'd just had lunch.

"Well, no, but—"

"You don't want to outstay your welcome as a couple, you know. Do try not to be a nuisance to Yuu. Like you were back then." Yuu paled when she said this. "You really must come back home soon, the two of you, and get back on with your lives. I'm sure you agree, don't you, Tomoya?"

"Ah . . ." my husband answered vaguely and took a big bite out of a dumpling, as if even being polite was too much bother.

"Well, I only came today to see how you were getting on. Mom's worried about you too. Staying here in this house with Yuu, of all people."

"I'm sorry. Perhaps I should have gone away for a while," Yuu hurriedly apologized. Maybe he felt awkward about the way my husband and I were sitting there, mindlessly letting her words go in one ear and out the other.

"It's not your fault, Yuu. Haven't the villagers said anything? I'm worried these two may be causing trouble."

From the tone of her voice, it was clear that my sister was not speaking for herself but on behalf of society. I envied her ability to do that.

My niece was just beginning to get bored of playing in the house when my sister stood up. "Well, it's time we were getting back," she said.

"Oh, won't you stay a little longer?" my husband said as he quickly stood up and slid open the living room door, eagerly ushering her out. "What a pity you have to go so soon," he said several times as he placed her shoes ready for her to put on.

"I'll come again."

My sister seemed very well aware that my husband didn't like her. She left the house without even reproaching him for the way he sent her packing.

I accompanied her as far as her car. "Did you drive up that mountain road yourself?"

"Yes, I did."

"Ah, you're a good driver! You always used to get so carsick on that road."

"By the way, you know those people handing out leaflets at the station are in the news again?"

This was so out of the blue that for a moment I didn't know what she was talking about.

"You remember not long ago that high school student in the neighboring town who was brutally murdered and his killer arrested? The talk shows are saying that there are similarities with Mr. Igasaki's case, even though that happened over twenty years ago. So his parents have started handing out leaflets again. Normally a family would move out of a house where such a terrible thing happened, but they haven't. Even the neighborhood association commented on that. There's a rumor going about that his parents themselves are the murderers and hid the evidence. It's really awful!"

"Wow!"

"You used to hand out leaflets for them too, didn't you? How about helping out again?"

"Hmm, I'll think about it."

I watched her car pull off into the distance before sluggishly making my way back to the house.

My husband was in the altar room yelling, "Aaarrghhh!!! The bastards! They finally came." He tripped over my bedding and had to grab on to my shoulder to stop himself falling. "She's been completely brainwashed by the Factory. I'll never be able to just be myself. And it's all their fault!"

"Calm down, Tomoya. My sister can't force us to go back. All she can do is put a bit of pressure on us like she did just now. We can still stay here for a while yet."

"Did you see that woman's eyes? She's crazy! It's like she thinks we're criminals, and she's just letting us get away with it for the time being. Why do I have to have her permission to be who I am? Who does she think she is?"

Yuu had watched this outburst in astonishment, but finally he collected himself. Laying a hand on my husband's back, he said, "Calm down, will you? Anyway, it's getting chilly. Let's go and sit in the kotatsu, shall we?"

"Yeah, all right." my husband said, looking sheepish.

As he soothed my husband, Yuu seemed preoccupied.

* * *

That night, while my husband was in the bath, I was on the veranda gazing at the stars when Yuu slid the shoji open and asked, "Aren't you cold sitting out there?"

"I have a hot water bottle to keep warm."

"I see."

He sat down next to me. This was unusual I thought. Normally he went out of his way to avoid being alone with me whenever my husband was out of sight.

"Um . . . this might sound strange coming from me, but does Tomoya know what happened between us when were kids?"

"We've never really talked about the past. He's my partner, but that doesn't mean we're friends."

"It's best to talk about that sort of thing with a partner. If he finds out later it might lead to a misunderstanding, and he'll probably feel hurt."

"What sort of misunderstanding?"

Yuu looked taken aback by my question. "That there is, er . . . a relationship between you and me."

"Yuu, you're acting like someone in a TV drama. Of course there's a relationship between us. We're cousins."

"This isn't a drama. It's real life. If you are misunderstood, Natsuki, you'll be even more cut off from the Factory. Anyone who contravenes their logic will be punished."

"Tomoya is all right. He's an even more ardent believer in Planet Popinpobopia than I am."

Yuu sighed. "Natsuki, we aren't children anymore. That kind of crazy reasoning won't work. You have to do better. As an adult, you have to squarely face up to problems."

"What problems? Do better than what? Look, Yuu, I already explained it clearly to you. I told you about Tomoya and me. You're just not listening. You're too busy tuning into society's noise. However much we talk, it's just meaningless babble to you."

I looked up at him. He had grown a little taller than me.

"Lucky you," I went on. "You've been completely brainwashed, haven't you? The sooner I am too, the better. I'm not like Tomoya. I don't yearn for an alien eye. I want to get an Earthling perspective, and as soon as possible. It would make everything so much easier."

Yuu sighed. "You haven't changed a bit, have you, Natsuki? It's really like you're frozen in time."

Yuu despised me. But there was nothing I could do about that. The alien eye had already been downloaded into me. It was the only way I could see the world.

"I'll talk to Tomoya tomorrow. Since you say it's that important, I'll follow the Earthling rules. It's not as though I'm trying to rebel," I told him, hugging the hot water bottle tightly to me. It was only lukewarm.

* * *

The next morning over breakfast, I told Tomoya that there was something I wanted to talk to him about. Before I could go any further, he said happily, "Me too. I'm going to try having sex with my grandfather."

Yuu choked, spraying miso soup over the kotatsu.

"Why?" I asked my husband, handing some tissues and a dishcloth to Yuu.

"Incest isn't very common, is it? It's taboo. Therefore I can use it as a step toward liberating myself from the brainwashing."

"Hmm, you think so?" I was skeptical. His idea was rooted in a human sense of values, and I couldn't help thinking it was a typically human concept.

"I want to try whatever people find most taboo. Other than murder."

"Hold on a moment," Yuu said, flustered. "How can I put this . . . ? Anyway, sex without consent is a crime."

"It's all right. Tomoya's grandfather is in a vegetative state in the hospital."

"That's even worse!"

"Why?" I looked Yuu in the eye. "That sort of thing happens everywhere, you know. We just don't see it. Even now, someone somewhere in the world is being used as a tool. It'll happen again today too. That's all it is."

"Natsuki, what you are talking about is a crime. It's abnormal."

"So what? Adults are expected to turn a blind eye to anything abnormal, aren't they? That's the way it is. Why so virtuous now? You're just a regular adult, after all. All you have to do is ignore it, just like any other regular adult."

I had no intention of condemning the crime my husband was planning to commit. If he wanted so much to become an alien, that was fine by me. And if he wanted to injure someone with his testes, then he should go right ahead I thought. If he actually went through with it, then at least he could become a monster. When I tried to imagine it, my hands shook, and there was a loud buzzing like a cicada in my right ear.

"There's some truth in what you're saying, Yuu," he said. "Now that I think about it, of course it would be a crime. It's just I thought that my grandfather wouldn't realize, so I wouldn't be prosecuted for it. That was wrong of me."

"Why?" I asked coolly, feeling my fingertips trembling. "What is crime, anyway? Earthlings are always doing it, right? They're forever carrying out crimes without any qualms at all."

"Ah. You've got a point there, Natsuki. You *are* from Planet Popinpobopia, after all," he said. "Mom is really busy with caregiving and doesn't have time for anything else, so I'll try out incest with my brother. Of course, I'll explain it to him properly and get his consent."

"Hold on. What do you hope to achieve with this?" Yuu asked.

My husband looked at him strangely. "To become an alien, of course. How many times do I have to explain that to you?"

"But even if you *do* do something like that, it won't change the fact that you're human."

"I won't know until I try. Anyway, I want to give it a go. I want to discard my humanity before I'm dragged back to the Factory." My husband's gaze turned to me. "I'm sorry, Natsuki. I've been doing all the talking. What was it you wanted to talk about?"

"Well, when Yuu and I were in elementary school, we thought we were lovers, and we even once had sex. We held a secret wedding ceremony too."

My husband sighed. "I can't believe you're worried about something like that, Natsuki. I suppose the Factory must be getting to you after all. I'm quite disappointed I must say."

"Um, it was me who told Natsuki to tell you about it. Sorry," Yuu hastily butted in. "I thought you would have a hard time of it should there be any misunderstanding."

"Hard time of it? Really? Well, from my point of view, it's you who's having a hard time of it," my husband said, peering at Yuu in concern. "You're lucky enough to be living in an abandoned factory, but here you are still apparently under the Factory's spell. But never mind, someday you, too, will be able to download the alien eye."

Yuu was staring at my husband with narrowed eyes, although I couldn't say whether this was because he found the light too bright, was being hostile toward him, or simply felt sleepy.

My husband stopped eating his rice and, still holding his bowl, continued, "You see, that's when you'll be able to see the real world, the pure world that your eyes are really seeing, unsullied by your brain. That perspective will be the greatest gift from us as a couple to you."

Yuu opened his mouth ready to argue back, but no words came out, and he just sat there staring vacantly, as though swallowed up by the force of my husband's gaze.

"Yuu, I thank you from the bottom of my heart," my husband went on. "I am truly grateful to you for letting us come and take refuge here. I want to return the favor. I just hope we have enough time to do that before we're forced to go back to the Factory."

He put his bowl down and looked alternately at me and Yuu. "At any rate, I'm going to go to my parents' place this weekend. I will have sex with someone in my family before coming back here. Of course with their consent and without hurting anyone. If all goes well, I want you to celebrate my success. If I can have both of your blessings, I believe I will feel very happy."

"Okay," I said. Despite my husband's calm explanation, my fingertips wouldn't stop trembling.

That night I couldn't sleep. There was still a buzzing sound in my right ear.

My mouth had remained broken all the way through school. I couldn't taste anything, so I lost a lot of weight. Everyone around me was gradually beginning to function as components of the Baby Factory, while I found myself being left behind. Before they knew it, they had all been brainwashed.

My classmates all longed to fall in love, and they began to try hard to be the sort of girls suited to romance.

"Why?" they would ask me when I said there wasn't anyone I fancied. All the other girls liked talking about boys. They were concerned if someone didn't join in.

I was looking for a church where I could confess. I wanted to take all the words out from inside my body and show them to someone. I chose someone of the same sex simply because I'd had absolutely no contact with any boys and didn't think they would understand me anyway. The sooner I could lay to rest the words within me the better.

When I was in senior high school, I summoned my courage and tried to talk to my friend Kanae. We were from the same neighborhood, we went to the same school, and we got along well. I also had the feeling that she would be less biased since she'd been to a different cram school.

"Kanae, do you remember when that teacher from the cram school by the station was murdered?"

"Oh, you mean that really cool teacher, right? I was in a different cram school, but I remember that. The poor guy."

"I was in his school."

"Really? Everyone there seemed really close. I remember being so impressed seeing you all handing out leaflets together."

"But you know what? That teacher was a bit weird. I know you shouldn't speak ill of the dead, but . . ."

"What do you mean, weird?"

"Well . . ."

I plucked up my courage and told her what had happened. About the sanitary napkin, and about him putting his thing in my mouth, doing my best not to be too explicit.

Kanae pulled a face. "Ew, what is that? You're saying he was your boyfriend? Like, an elementary schoolgirl with a university student?"

"What? No! That's not what I meant . . . I mean, he was a pervert."

Kanae burst out laughing. "No way! Are you sure you didn't just dream it all? After all, you were only in elementary school back then. From what I saw of his photo on the news, he must have been really popular. Sounds like a fantasy to me."

"No, you've got it all wrong. I hated him."

"If you didn't like it, you should have told him! It's your fault for not turning him down. Apart from anything, if you hated him so much, you shouldn't have gone to his house, right?"

"Well no, but—"

"Even if it's true . . . After all, he was so cool you must have purposely let down your guard. That's basically consenting, isn't it? I can't understand why you're playing the tragic heroine, really."

"No, you're wrong. It wasn't like that at all."

Kanae heaved a big sigh. "Well, look, just what is it you want me to say? Why are you telling me? It's such a turnoff!"

She kept her distance after that. Another friend told me that she was going around telling everyone I was a liar.

The second time I came out about it was when I was in university, and my friend Miho told me that she was often groped on the train. This time I cautiously chose someone who was also a victim for my confession.

I was worried she might accuse me of lying like Kanae had, but I steeled myself and this time described what happened as a criminal act without bothering to sugarcoat it. I hid the fact that he was dead and any other information that might arouse any sympathy for him and carefully selected just the episodes that might gain sympathy for myself. Everything I said was true, but apparently I'd given Miho the impression that Mr. Igasaki was not a good-looking young student but a fat and ugly middle-aged man. That made it much more relatable for her.

"What the hell? That is just so gross, an old man like that. You poor thing, Natsuki!"

I was relieved that she was so enraged. However, when I entered my second year of college, then my third, and still made hardly any effort to meet boys, her focus began to shift.

"Look, I know what you went through was awful, but aren't you letting him win? Finding happiness is the best revenge. The longer you continue to mope, the longer that dirty old man will be rejoicing."

"Yeah." I always agreed with her.

"Look," she went on, I hate to be the one to say this, but he didn't even force you to go all the way, did he? So I kind of wonder why you're acting so traumatized. I mean, I've been groped loads and it's horrible, but we just have to put up with it, right? If we let that sort of thing stop us from hooking up with anyone for our whole lives, the human race will die out pretty quick! Some of my friends suffered way worse, and they all have boyfriends now. Everyone else does their best to forget the past and look to the future, Natsuki. You've got as far as college without even so much as speaking to a boy. It's a bit weird."

She was probably right, but I just laughed it off.

One day I went to meet Miho only to find she wasn't alone. There was a guy with her.

"Who is he?" I asked.

"Someone I want to introduce you to." She laughed and turned to the boy. "I'm sorry, she's got issues with men. But hey, you said you liked the innocent type, right? I thought the two of you would be just right for each other."

I was glaring at Miho without moving a muscle. The boy looked a bit scared.

"Who is he?" I repeated.

I no longer knew who Miho was or why she was making such a fuss or why was she so determined to get me to have sex with someone.

Furious, I walked away. Behind me I heard the boy laugh and say, "I know I said I'd prefer a virgin to used goods, but that's too much!"

I was keenly aware that I was unable to fulfill my duty as a tool for the Baby Factory. Being a Popinpobopian, I just couldn't understand Earthlings. On Earth, young women were supposed to fall in love and have sex, and if they didn't, they were "lonely" or "bored" or "wasting their youth and would regret it later!"

"You have to make up for lost time," Miho was always telling me.

But I couldn't understand why, when it meant doing something I didn't want to do.

We would soon be dispatched to the Factory. Those who were already prepared would guide those who weren't yet ready. Miho was my guide.

Earthlings baffled me. If I were an Earthling, though, I suppose it would be absolutely natural for me to be controlled by my genes, too, just like Miho was. It must be a peaceful, secure way of life.

It was just before Christmas, decorations and ornamental trees adorned the streets, and there was romance in the air.

Society was a system for falling in love. People who couldn't fall in love had to fake it. What came first: the system or love? All I knew was that love was a mechanism designed to make Earthlings breed.

I took a train back to Mirai New Town. At the ticket gates, I saw Mr. Igasaki's parents handing out leaflets. People walking past were ignoring their grief-stricken faces and pleas for information, casually avoiding taking the leaflets urged on them by the aging couple. They had attracted a lot of sympathy at the time of the murder, but now they were treated as a nuisance, like foreign matter in the town.

I quietly averted my eyes, hoping they wouldn't see me, and headed for home.

Humans got really worked up when an organism that had inherited their genes was killed. Even now, Mr. Igasaki's parents were still driven by grief and rage.

Unlike when I was little, there was now a shopping mall and retail outlets around the station and the area was bustling with people. There were lots of families out walking among all the Christmas decorations and couples in school uniforms holding hands.

The Factory seemed to be putting more and more effort into promoting how wonderful it was to fall in love and how fabulous it was to produce a human at the end of that.

In my belly I already had a womb primed for this Baby Factory. I was getting to the age where I would soon be censured for not letting this organ be used for the benefit of the Factory.

The next morning I awoke to find my husband already dressed and ready to go out.

"Won't you have breakfast before you go?"

"No, I've already called a taxi. I'll only be gone one night. I want to carry my plan out as quickly as possible and come back here."

"I see. Good luck!"

My husband had just left when Yuu came downstairs.

"Where's Tomoya?"

"He's gone already."

"What, already? I told him I'd give him a lift!"

"He's a bit reckless."

Yuu sighed. "Okay, well I'll leave, too, after breakfast."

"Where are you going?"

"I'll go down the mountain and stay in a hotel tonight."

"What? Why?"

"Surely even you can understand why we two shouldn't spend the night here together on our own?"

Evidently everything we'd told him had washed over him. He was only listening to the voice of society. Yuu's propriety was, to me, proof that his brainwashing was complete. I envied him.

"I'll go. I'm the freeloader here, after all."

"But you can't drive, Natsuki. There's only one bus a day, so it's simplest if I go," he said irritably and went to the washroom.

Given that my husband and I were causing Yuu so much trouble, the least I could do was prepare breakfast I thought. I was just on my way to the kitchen when I heard a car pull up outside. I went to see who it was, thinking my husband had probably forgotten something, to see an unfamiliar orange vehicle.

A suntanned man got out. Noticing me, he approached with a dubious look on his face.

"Yota?" The name came to mind the moment I saw his face. He was Uncle Teruyoshi's eldest son, one of the kids I'd run around with during the summer here.

"Natsuki?" He looked surprised.

I nodded.

"What are you doing here?"

"I came with my husband to stay a while."

"What about Yuu?"

"He's inside."

Yota looked troubled.

Just then Yuu came out. "Hey, Yota!" he called, looking relieved. "Good timing. Will you have breakfast? I'm going out straight afterward."

"Sure, but what about Natsuki's husband?"

"You just missed him. Some business came up in Tokyo, and he won't be back tonight, so I thought it best to go down to the valley to stay in a hotel."

"Yes, that seems best. But what's up with him? For all that you two are cousins, going out and leaving you alone together . . . That's not normal, is it? Surely he should have taken Natsuki with him?"

"That's what I thought too," Yuu said, looking reassured.

Yota's sense of propriety seemed to resonate with Yuu, and this enabled them to really connect with each other deeply I thought. Yuu looked far more relaxed than I'd seen him until now.

Yuu smoothly explained my husband's sudden absence, replacing the provocative word "incest" with other words such as "work."

"Well, I guess if that's the case, it can't be helped," Yota said, apparently more or less satisfied. "How about staying at my place, Yuu? Paying for a hotel is a waste of money."

"Well, if you don't mind."

Yota lived in Ueda with his wife and children. I was impressed by how well he was functioning as a Factory component.

"I'm sorry that I was a bit sharp with you earlier, Natsuki," he said. "You know, after, er . . . what happened, the relatives stopped gathering together here for the summer. I had no idea why, and I really missed being here. Then when Granny died, everyone came again, except you. When I asked why you weren't there, Dad told me I was old enough to know what had happened and explained what you'd done that night after Grandpa's funeral. To be honest, I was shocked and disgusted."

Yuu nodded as he listened to Yota. He somehow looked pleased, even though he was being told he himself was disgusting. There was no trace of the uneasy expression he wore when he was around me and my husband; he looked as though he had recovered his self-confidence. Normality was contagious, and exposure to the infection was necessary to keep up with it. Yota was probably supplying him with some of the same strain of normality as his own for the first time in a while.

"Since Yuu started living here, this place has been on my mind, and I've been dropping by occasionally. And then meeting you again after all this time, Natsuki, somehow those days came back to me, and I got the jitters."

"I know, I know," Yuu said, eagerly pouring more tea for Yota.

"Hadn't you two met up since then?"

"No, we hadn't been in contact at all since that night," Yuu answered immediately.

"I don't suppose you could," Yota said with some emotion. "Your mom stopped visiting after that. After all, she was practically disowned by the family. I only found out about her suicide at her funeral."

"She committed suicide?" I was shocked. My sister hadn't told me how she'd died.

"Didn't you know?" Yota asked, staring at me.

"Nobody told you anything either, I suppose?"

"No . . ."

"After that all the relatives fell apart, you know. I really think what we did was wrong," Yuu muttered.

"Wrong? I suppose that's how you see it, Yuu."

"Anyone would!" Yuu looked me in the eye. "We were wrong."

I gulped and was about to make a retort when Yota changed the subject and in a bright voice said, "But look how run-down Granny's house is! The tatami floor in the altar room is looking all worn."

"It really is! I can hardly believe that all us cousins used to play here in the living room."

"It's true!"

Yuu and I both chimed in.

"We always had fireworks in the garden every summer, didn't we?"

"Wow, it's all like a dream now."

Yuu narrowed his eyes as if trying to remember. "You always got told off for taking two sparklers, didn't you, Yota?"

"Yeah, those things were so lame. Remember how Dad always used to launch some big rockets for us too?"

"And those parachutes . . . remember how we used to fight over them too?"

Together we talked about our memories of that time. In the other world of the past, we really had all sat on this veranda eating watermelon. That was something you never saw these days.

The three of us had breakfast together, then Yota and Yuu drove down the mountain.

Yota was concerned about me. "Will you be okay here on your own, Natsuki?" he asked. "Do you want to come with us? You can sleep in my wife's room."

"She doesn't have her husband's permission," Yuu said immediately. "It wouldn't be right."

He glared at me disdainfully. People can easily pass judgment on others when they're protected by their own normality.

"I'll sleep here alone," I told Yota.

* * *

My husband returned soon after lunch the following day. I was lazing around in the kotatsu when I heard the front door open, and he came in looking pale.

"Hi Tomoya, how was it?"

"They're after me. I have to hide right now."

Before I could get any more information from my trembling husband, there was the sound of a car pulling up. He shrieked. I hid him in the kitchen and went outside to find not his pursuer but Yuu getting unhurriedly out of his car.

"I saw a taxi and thought it must be Tomoya's. Is he back?"

"Well—"

Before I could answer, there was the sound of yet another car outside. When I nervously went to see who it was, this time I found a big black car.

A glowering figure alighted from the driver's seat. I grabbed Yuu's hand and hurriedly pulled him into the house, locking the door behind us.

"What shall we do, Yuu? It's an envoy from the Factory chasing Tomoya."

"Envoy?"

My husband huddled in the kitchen.

Before long, the glowering figure loomed behind the frosted glass in the door.

"Tomoya! Come on out. I know you're in there!"

"Who is it?" Yuu whispered in my ear.

"Tomoya's father."

Yuu's eyes widened. "In that case, we have to invite him in. We can't just turn him away, you know."

He turned to the door. "Hold on a moment, sir! I'm the current resident of this house. I'll open up right away."

He opened the door to see my father-in-law standing there, his face and neck tinged crimson with rage.

"Excuse me, but is my son here?" my father-in-law demanded courteously, before pushing his way in and storming through the house yelling "Tomoya!"

Eventually he dragged my husband out of the kitchen. "You stupid brat!"

It's like a TV drama I thought as I watched him beating my husband. As a child, I'd often been amused by drama series, however serious the theme. Seeing one now being played out right before my very eyes, acted with such deep conviction, I almost burst out laughing.

"Come on, let's keep things calm, shall we?"

Yuu was a good actor, too, playing the part of someone desperately trying to get a father to calm down and stop beating his son. He blended completely into the scene being brought to life by my father-in-law.

"Stop, please! Help!" my husband screamed pathetically, making a dash for where I stood as Yuu held my father-in-law back.

"Do you really want me to save you?" There was a grass-cutting scythe by the front door. "Do you, Tomoya? If you really want me to save you, then I will do my very best."

My husband realized what was in my line of sight and quickly shook his head. "No, no, actually I don't really want you to help me."

"Really? Okay, fine."

I watched as my father-in-law shook off Yuu and again grabbed my husband, resuming the family drama. "Stop! Someone help me!" my husband screamed. "You worthless piece of shit!" my father-in-law roared, absorbed in his script as he began beating my husband again.

One of my husband's teeth flew out and landed at my feet. It was covered in blood. I picked up the bloody tooth and put it in my pocket.

"Please stop!" Yuu implored. "Calm down!" There at my husband's side, he was playing the part of the wife better than I was.

Putting together what my father-in-law was yelling, my husband had actually gone to his elder brother's house and, with all sincerity, proposed committing an incestuous act with him. He had apparently fervently explained that by not having a romantic relationship but instead committing an incestuous act, he might be able to become something nonhuman.

My brother-in-law worried that he might be involved with a religious cult and secretly recorded their conversation on his iPhone as he tried to soothe him and treated him to a meal. When my husband got drunk and fell asleep on the sofa, my brother-in-law went to see their father to ask for advice on how to handle the situation. My husband was then woken from sleep by a furious phone call from his father and in a panic fled back to Akishina by bullet train then taxi. My father-in-law had contacted my parents, who gave him the address in Akishina, and he had easily caught up with his son.

Once my father-in-law had finished beating my husband, he dragged us outside and pushed us into his car. "Both of you, you should know better at your age. Pathetic!" he said, stepping angrily on the gas.

I was being returned to the Factory, just like I had been that summer's day in my childhood. The normal people were once again bringing me back to that town.

I glanced out of the window and saw Yuu standing rooted to the spot outside the storehouse staring after us openmouthed.

His figure rapidly receded into the distance as the car sped off.

CHAPTER 6

Back in the Factory, a third-degree interrogation was awaiting us.

My husband's parents had been in touch with my parents, and we were immediately separated for cross-examination. My husband was hauled off to his parents' house in Tokyo, and I was delivered to my parents' house in Mirai New Town in Chiba.

I'd been kind of hoping I could finally get them to brainwash me, but for the sake of my husband I maintained my silence. Every day I was interrogated by Mom and Dad and often by my sister, too, but I kept my mouth shut.

"You're so stubborn, Natsuki," Mom said with a sigh.

One night, a week after the interrogations first started, Mom produced a bottle of brandy and, with cloying overfamiliarity, invited me to sit with her.

"Fancy a drink?"

"No, I'm fine," I said.

"Don't be like that! Now and then it's good for us women to have a drink and talk. Don't you agree?" she insisted, pouring some brandy over ice.

I had rarely seen Mom touch alcohol, but from the way she started in on it eagerly I thought she was actually probably quite good at holding her drink. Reluctantly I took a sip from the glass placed in front of me. I couldn't taste it, but I liked the cold sensation from the ice.

After a while Mom blurted out, "I met up with Tomoya's parents recently, and they told me that you two aren't, er, intimate with each other."

I was taken aback. I'd never expected my husband to spill the beans about our particular marital arrangement.

"It really won't do, you know. That sort of thing is so important for a couple. I've seen on TV that some young people are, um, intimate a lot at first and stop later, but from what I hear you two haven't even done it once."

I heard a rattling and glanced down at my hand to see that it was shaking. It felt strange to see my fingertips trembling like that.

"And it's a wife's duty to be intimate, you know. Tomoya finds it hard to hold down a job, doesn't he? You have to support him in that regard, Natsuki. You're his wife!"

My body was not my own. I had always been secretly shirking the role I had been assigned as a tool of society.

The time had come for me to be taken to task for this, I thought.

I had been half resigned to and half longing for the day when the Earthlings would gang up and brainwash me. But I had never imagined that time would come so soon or in this form.

When I said I wanted to talk to my husband, Mom looked pleased.

"I'm sure you do. You've already been apart for a week now, and you are a couple, after all." She rubbed my back. "You understand what I'm saying, don't you? Make sure you get intimate with him, all right? Tomoya's a late developer, so you'll have to guide him and show him what to do. Teach him the basics. As casually as you can and tactfully, too, so as not to hurt his pride. That's the duty of a charming wife, you know!"

The next day I went to my husband's parents' place in Setagaya and rang the doorbell. My mother-in-law opened the door to me, all smiles.

"Natsuki, how nice to see you. Your parents called. They said you could stay here tonight, then tomorrow you can both go home together."

I was shown through to the living room and together we drank tea.

"What about Tomoya . . . ?"

"Ah. Well, you might be a bit shocked when you see him."

The living room door slid open and my father-in-law came in. Behind him was my husband. It appeared he had been quite severely beaten, with bruises on his face and arms, and his hair had been cropped like a monk's.

My father-in-law glowered at me. "So you're here," he said. "What the hell are you and Tomoya up to? You haven't done it even once! That's worse than being barren."

"Oh really, you mustn't use that word. It's considered discriminatory these days," my mother-in-law admonished him as she poured him some tea. "Natsuki's a new type of woman from a younger generation. You really must be more considerate you know." She smiled at me.

"You know very well how much I hate people who insist on their rights while neglecting their duty," he said irritably and took a sip of the tea. "Too bitter. Pour it again."

My mother-in-law forced a smile and put some more hot water into the teapot. "If you speak to her like that, she'll become even more stubborn, won't she now?" she said, her eyes on me.

"Anyway, you two get going and produce a child. If you won't have relations, then annul the marriage. You're abnormal, the both of you."

"That's up to us to decide," my monk-headed husband said in a small voice.

My mother-in-law sighed. "Look, Tomoya. Do it a lot and make a family, then once the relationship has cooled, you play around outside the marriage. That's the way it is for lots

of couples, isn't it? Playing around is a man's reward. Your
father has had his fair share, haven't you dear? But really, not
even doing it at all from the start, that's not what marriage is
about, is it now?"

"In Los Angeles, a lack of marital relations is considered a fine reason for divorce, you know. How about trying
counseling?"

Just why Los Angeles had suddenly been brought into it
I didn't know. My father-in-law was now sipping the fresh tea
my mother-in-law had poured for him, his face grave.

"That's right. You too, Natsuki. You married into our family, and if you don't fulfill your duty as a wife, you'll be causing
problems for us."

"You're out of your minds," my husband muttered.

That night, when I woke up to go to the bathroom, I
overheard my mother- and father-in-law talking.

"At her age, is she even still getting periods? Won't they
have stopped by now?"

"Oh really, dear. Her periods should be fine. She is getting
a bit old to give birth for the first time, though."

"Wouldn't it be better to split them up and find him a
new wife?"

"The thing is, Tomoya has always been a difficult child.
He's a late developer too. Maybe we should give it a year and
see how things go. If she isn't pregnant by then, we can think
about what to do. Unlike women, men can start a family later
in life as long as their partner is young."

Being treated crudely as a tool for society was clearer than all that talk of falling in love, and actually I wasn't upset by it at all. I even began to feel vindicated. My parents-in-law were revealing that beneath the usual Baby Factory tendency to sugar-coat everything the objective was simply to manufacture babies.

My husband was far more disturbed by his parents' attitude. He again went out of his way to defend me at breakfast.

"Natsuki is really special. There's only one of her kind on Earth."

"My, my, you are very attached to her, aren't you?" his mother said. "Hmm. I'd say she's certainly especially strange." She tittered and put some rice into my husband's bowl.

I tittered too, and she looked at me with repugnance.

Her womb and my father-in-law's testes were tools too. They were ruled by their genes, yet they were aglow with pride—and even that pride was under the control of the Factory. I was amused by how cute these poor Earthling creatures were.

I wasn't bothered about being treated as a tool by other tools. I was far more weirded out by the strange way my parents and sister had started fawning on me.

"I do understand how you feel, Natsuki. I was like that too when I was younger," Mom said.

My sister nodded. "Yes, me too! But when you have a baby of your own, you'll wonder how anything so adorable could possibly exist!"

Both Mom and my sister kept going on and on about how wonderful motherhood was, as if it were some kind of religion. I was still hoping to be brainwashed. But repeating "motherhood is wonderful" over and over like a Buddhist chant was hardly going to be enough to brainwash me on its own. It just made me feel uncomfortable. I listened to them both saying how much they understood me, wishing they would come up with something more effective.

After hours of being made to listen to all their talk, my husband and I were finally released from the cross-examination and allowed to go back to our own home.

"Ugh, that was awful!" my husband groaned. I sighed, and he hung his head apologetically. "It was all my fault that you got subjected to that interrogation too. I'm really sorry."

"That's okay. I'm an alien, so this sort of thing is nothing for me. But what about you, Tomoya. Are you okay?"

He nodded, but he looked pale. He probably wouldn't be able to take much more of this I thought.

That weekend, Shizuka invited me out for dinner. My husband said he was going to meet an old classmate from elementary school, too, so we each went out to our separate evenings.

I'd already come home and was lounging around on the sofa when I heard a noise from the front door.

"Hi there, is that you?"

"Yes, I'm back." My husband came in looking like thunder.

Seeing the look on his face I had a gut instinct. "I don't suppose the Factory has been on your case?"

"You too, Natsuki?"

I nodded. Both my husband and I had been called up by old friends and had been excited about going out to meet them, but it had all been a trap set by the Factory.

Shizuka's husband had agreed to babysit while we went out to dinner at an Italian restaurant in the shopping mall next to the station.

"Actually, Natsuki, your mom asked me to do this," Shizuka had started, and my heart sank.

I don't have many friends, and I was happy when she'd invited me out. I'd felt exhilarated after having been released from interrogation and had gone in high spirits, but it turned out that she was colluding with my parents.

"I'm saying this because I'm your friend, Natsuki, but it really is strange, you know. You don't even do all the housework when you're not working, do you? From what you'd said, I always thought your husband was so good at helping you out. But I had no idea you dealt with everything completely separately: the cooking, laundry, cleaning, everything! Sharing tasks is fine but dividing them up is weird. It's like having a roommate! That's not marriage, is it? And I was really shocked to hear that you haven't been intimate with each other even once!"

Now it was my turn to be shocked. How on earth did Shizuka even know about our nonexistent sex life? Previously she hadn't noticed a thing and had even suspected I was pregnant. I didn't know whether she'd been talking with my mom or my sister, but I wondered just how much information about us as a couple they'd exchanged. If they ever found out about the surinuke dot com website, we would probably be forced to split up I thought with a shiver.

But it appeared Shizuka didn't know how we'd met. Perhaps it had been one of my husband's friends who had let it slip. I'd heard that his friend had found out about the division of housework and had called me a toxic wife. Perhaps that was how Shizuka had gotten hold of that information, although I couldn't be sure.

"It's only after couples get intimate the first time that they really become a couple I think."

Why were all the Earthlings calling sex being intimate all of a sudden? They probably infected each other with their words.

"I mean, look, if you really can't get intimate with each other, I think it's probably better to split up, you know. For the both of you. A couple that doesn't get intimate, it's abnormal."

I put in the occasional "uh-huh" and "I guess" here and there and kept glancing at the clock, wondering how long it would be before I could go home to our condo.

It was apparently the same with my husband; his friend was in collusion with the Factory and had given him a merciless lecture. He sighed and covered his face with his hands.

"Why do we have to go through this? We were happy enough living together as we were." He sank down onto the sofa, holding his head in his hands. "We're being watched. People from the Factory are keeping an eye on us. There's no escape."

"On Earth, it seems that couples have to mate, doesn't it?"

"I can deal with having to work. But I don't want to mate. If I mated with you, we wouldn't be ourselves anymore."

"But our bodies aren't our own. They belong to society. We're tools of society, so if we don't mate we'll be persecuted."

"But *why*? It's my body!"

"Because those are the rules of the Factory. We're slaves to our genes."

My husband went still, his face turned downward. Maybe he was weeping.

The doorbell rang. Probably a delivery or maybe another envoy from the Factory.

The next morning my sister called saying she wanted to talk and I should meet her in the karaoke box near the station shopping mall. I was sick of being called up and given sermons, but she said, "It's something I can't say when Mom's around," so reluctantly I went to meet her.

I was always careful not to let anyone use my phone, but maybe she'd gotten wind of us having used the surinuke dot com site another way.

If she ever told my parents-in-law, it would probably mean the end of our marriage. My sister was a great believer in romantic love, so somehow I had to convince her that I did actually "love" my husband. This was what was going through my mind as I sat down with her in the private room. I had just taken a sip of oolong tea when she came out with something totally unexpected.

"Look, I know all about it. Why you can't be intimate, Natsuki," she said. She went on, almost casually, "Back when you were in cram school, the teacher fiddled with you, didn't he?"

My throat constricted and I couldn't breathe. "Why . . . How . . . ?"

"I saw you. The day of the festival, you were late so I went to find you, and I saw you being taken by a man into a house. I was worried, so I went into the garden and looked inside. And you and your teacher were kissing."

Had we kissed? My memory of that time was hazy, and I couldn't say for certain that we hadn't.

"At the time, I thought how lucky you were," she went on.

"*Lucky?*" I repeated stupidly.

"I mean, you were still just a child, but you'd been chosen by that gorgeous man from such a good university. I was so jealous! I believed that people could only fall in love when God allowed them to. I was ugly, fat, and hairy, the laughing-stock of the whole school, so I wasn't allowed to fall in love. It was different for you, wasn't it Natsuki? Not just Cousin Yuu, but even an adult man had fallen in love with you. I was so incredibly jealous."

I didn't know what she was talking about.

"You know I always believed that however wretched and miserable I was, someday a Prince Charming would find me, like Cinderella. But back then, nobody even looked at me. God wouldn't allow me to fall in love." Then her tone changed. "That teacher died, didn't he? Did you kill him?"

"Don't be crazy!" I said immediately.

My sister nodded. "I guess it's crazy. Still, Natsuki, you were just a child and didn't know how lucky you were to have someone fall in love with you, so I just wondered. After all, you were still in elementary school. I don't suppose you would have been able to kill an adult man."

"A child wouldn't be capable of that. Some pervert killed him. That's what they said on the news."

I did my best to keep my voice calm, but the end of my words trembled slightly. It was almost ominous the way my sister kept smiling as she crossed and uncrossed her legs. Unusually for her, she was wearing a skirt. She peered into my face.

"Right. Supposing it were true, though, I would have had to do everything in my power to cover for you, Natsuki. Being the sister of a murderer, nobody would ever have fallen for me. Life would be over for a woman like that."

She smiled, and I saw saliva glistening on some lipstick stuck to her front teeth. Even as an adult, my sister entrusted the keys of her life to other people. Didn't that scare her? How could she be so cheerful?

"But Natsuki, you can't go on like this. I have to harden my heart to say this to you, but you won't be allowed to carry on running away. You have to get intimate, have a baby, and live a decent life."

"Who? Who won't allow me?"

"Everyone. The whole planet," she answered simply. "You know, I found adolescence really hard too. But now that I'm married, for the first time I'm able to lead a worthwhile existence. If my husband hadn't found me, I never would have known such happiness as a woman. I am really so fortunate that he fell for me. And I will not allow anything to destroy this happiness. Natsuki, you too, you have to forget the past and quickly find happiness as a woman. That's the most important thing for us as sisters."

Abruptly I put my hand over my right ear. I could hear a shrill, electronic buzzing. My sister's voice sounded far away, as though we were on the phone.

"Yuu seems to be turning respectable at last too. Right after you left, he told Uncle Teruyoshi that he was leaving the Akishina house. Now he's temporarily lodging at Uncle's place while he looks for a job and somewhere to live.

"Yuu is?"

So Yuu would also become a Baby Factory component, along with my husband and me, I thought vacantly as I listened to my sister's voice penetrate the electronic buzzing.

I went back home and opened the closet. I gently took out the tin box and lifted the lid. Piyyut was lying inside.

"Piyyut, answer me. Please!"

I was talking to Piyyut for the first time in twenty-three years, but he didn't answer.

"I want to use my magical powers once more. That was the Wicked Witch, right?"

Piyyut hadn't been washed for a long time, and his spines smelled moldy.

I crouched down holding him to me. He didn't make even the slightest movement. My trembling must have shaken the box on my lap, since the wire ring rattled inside it.

I must have fallen asleep like that. When I woke up, I was still wearing my clothes and makeup. I went out of my room to go wash my face and found my husband dressed in a suit, fixing his tie before the mirror.

"What's up? Are you going somewhere?"

"Good morning, Natsuki." His expression was stern. "I've decided to go along with the Factory. The first thing to do is find a job, so I'm going to Hello Work."

"Ah."

"Then I'm going to city hall to get divorce papers."

"Divorce papers?"

"Natsuki, I want us to split up." He turned to look at me, his tie still askew.

"Why?"

"It's all over for me. I've been trapped by the Factory. But you, you can still get away. I want you to cut loose and escape."

I opened my mouth to say something, but my husband stopped me, grabbing me hard by the shoulders.

"I know Yuu doubted whether you were really an alien. Maybe you do too. But you *are* Popinpobopian. You definitely are. I know it."

I looked up at him in surprise. His eyes were pitch-black, the color of space as seen from Akishina.

"You have to get free and escape the Factory alone. I will become its slave, and my life will be a living death. But I want you to survive. If you can live as a Popinpobopian, I'll be able to survive too."

My husband knew me better than I knew myself. It was true. Part of me did think I was actually an Earthling. Sometimes I thought being a Popinpobopian was effectively a mental illness that I had needed in order to protect myself, and the only way I would ever recover was by becoming a slave of the Factory. My husband knew that was what I thought.

"I . . . I probably killed someone once," I said, looking up at him.

He replied smoothly. "Really? But you're a Popinpobopian, after all. It's not much different from the way Earthlings kill mice. So what?" He sighed.

"Aren't you scared of me?"

He let go of my shoulders and resumed adjusting his tie. "What I'm really scared of is believing that the words society makes me speak are my own. You're different. That's how I know you're from another planet."

I threw my arms around him. He was surprised and stiffened, then he relaxed and stroked my back. I felt his body heat for the first time. It was low, and his chest and hands were cold.

I pulled away from him and declared, "I *am* Popinpobopian. And you are too. It's catching. Just like being an Earthling is infectious, and that's how people all become Earthlings. It's the same with our planet. So you're definitely a Popinpobopian by now." I took his cold hand in mine. "Let's escape together."

"Where to?"

"A village near the stars."

"In that case, let's take Yuu with us. If being Popinpobopian is catching, then he must have been infected. Let's go to Akishina, where Yuu's waiting."

"But he's not there anymore. He left the house right after we did and went to Uncle Teruyoshi's place. I never told you this, but actually he is Popinpobopian. He told me that when we were children. He's probably lost sight of it now, but he definitely is."

"What? In that case we have to save him!" my husband shouted. "If we don't, he'll be infected by the Earthlings!"

We quickly packed our bags and jumped in a taxi to the station.

"Do you know where your uncle lives, Natsuki?"

"Yeah, it's in my address book."

"Great. Let's head straight there!"

"How come you take Yuu so seriously?"

He tilted his head, as if he didn't understand the meaning of my question. "I mean, he took us in, didn't he? That's not all. He let me speak my own language. Earthlings probably don't realize it, but meeting someone like that is rare in life. That's a miracle in itself. I want to do something for him in return."

"Thank you." I squeezed his hand. "I'm so glad I came to this planet and married you."

Outside the window, the pure white Baby Factory raced by. Inside it, numerous breeding pairs were confined to their nests. They would multiply again today.

Uncle Teruyoshi's house wasn't far from the station.

As far as I could recall, this was only the second time I'd been there. It wasn't that he and Dad didn't get along, but my uncle was extremely sociable, so my taciturn father found it tiring to spend time with him and usually turned down invitations to go there on the way back from our Obon holiday. We stayed over only once when we couldn't get home because of a typhoon.

Even though we'd called out of the blue from the station, Uncle Teruyoshi had cheerfully told us to come right over.

He welcomed us in and showed us through to the living room, telling us, "Yuu's out shopping, but he'll be right back." The house felt bigger and quieter than I remembered. Last time my aunt had also been there, and there had been a lively atmosphere with Yota and his brothers running around, but Uncle Teruyoshi had been living alone since his wife's death.

Apparently Yuu had come straight here after leaving the Akishina house and was now lodging temporarily in what had been the children's bedroom.

"Yuu said he was going to look for a job and somewhere to live, but I put my foot down. I told him it wasn't going to be easy, so he should stay here for a while."

Yuu had first looked for a job in Nagano, but in the end he couldn't find anything suitable, so next week he was going to move to a studio apartment in Tokyo and attend interviews with several companies.

"Although I told him he should stick around here for a bit longer, there was no need to push himself. He's been through so much. I wanted him to feel free and happy. He's a good boy, that one."

As Uncle Teruyoshi talked, there came the sound of someone opening the front door.

"Ah, speak of the devil. That must be him now."

Yuu had apparently gone to buy a suit for his interviews. When he came into the living room and saw us there, his face hardened.

"They were worried about you, Yuu, and came especially to see you."

"Speaking of being worried, what about you two, Natsuki and Tomoya? How are things? Are you sure it's okay for you to be here?"

"We left the Factory today," my husband answered.

"Tomoya!" Yuu admonished, shooting him a warning look.

Uncle Teruyoshi seemed to think he was talking about an actual factory. "It's getting really tough in this recession, isn't it?" he said to my husband. "Well, I'm sure you've got lots to talk about, so I'll leave you to it. I have to take the dog out for his walk too. Take your time."

"People will think you're strange if you say such odd things," Yuu said after checking that Uncle Teruyoshi had gone. "And once they think you're strange, life will get really hard for you, you know." He sighed and sat down.

"Yuu, have you really left Akishina? We've escaped from the Factory and are thinking of going there to live full-time. Won't you escape with us? Do you really need to be a Baby Factory component?"

"Thanks for being so concerned about me, Tomoya. But I only ever intended to rest a while at that house. Like the summer holidays I enjoyed as a child. Actually, I think I stayed there a bit too long."

"But you're Popinpobopian!"

Yuu flinched. My husband leaned forward and grabbed his sleeve. "Natsuki told me everything. When you were a child, you arrived in a spaceship from Planet Popinpobopia. I wish you'd told me yourself."

"But that . . . It was just a silly childhood fantasy. It's not reality."

"What is reality? To me it looks like you're forcing yourself to become an Earthling."

Yuu looked down a moment, then raised his head and looked straight at us. "I hear orders in my head. Ever since I was a child, I could hear adults telling me what they wanted me to do, even though they didn't say it out loud. My mother especially was always telling me what to do without actually saying it. So I always automatically did as they said. I knew I had to in order to survive," he said flatly.

We watched him silently as he spoke. It must have been the first time I'd ever heard him say so much at once.

"After my mother died, I obeyed the voices of my college professors and other adults around me. When I went to work for the company, I obeyed the company voices. I lived my life unthinkingly obeying orders. When out of the blue I was told the company was virtually bankrupt and was being bought out, I did what the company wanted and resigned. But ever since then I've stopped hearing the commands that controlled my life. I no longer know what to do or how to live. Obeying those silent orders was how I had always survived."

My husband tightened his grip on Yuu's shirt. I worried about him wrinkling it, but Yuu didn't seem to notice as he went on, "That was when Uncle Teruyoshi suggested I take some time off and invited me to stay here in his house for a while. It occurred to me then that I wanted to go to the Akishina house again. But that's all over now. It's time for me to start hearing new orders. That's all."

My husband looked up at Yuu with a sad, angelic face, like an innocent child who has just been scolded. "But Yuu, then you'll be a tool for the Baby Factory. When really you're a Popinpobopian. And that's a wonderful thing to be."

Uneasily I asked Yuu in a small voice, "Was I also giving you silent orders?"

Yuu looked at me in surprise. "You, Natsuki? Well . . . it's true I always did hear a silent voice from you, but it wasn't anything like the orders I was getting from the adults. It was the sound of an SOS. That somehow drew me to you. I guess I thought we were similar. So it was my own choice to be with you, Natsuki."

"I see."

I felt relieved, but then Yuu had always been the sort of child to intuit what people wanted him to do. He'd probably said what he had just now because he'd felt that's what I'd wanted him to say.

"So, you're going to become an Earthling, just like that, are you, Yuu? Is that what you really want?"

"What I want?" Yuu looked doubtful. "It's not about what I want. I just want to survive."

If surviving meant taking his life forward into the future, he was making the right choice. There was nothing I could say to that. My husband stood up.

"I see. Well then, shall we at least hold a divorce ceremony?"

"Divorce ceremony?" Yuu repeated blankly, and I felt uneasy.

"When you and Natsuki were little, you held a marriage ceremony, didn't you? Natsuki and I also got married. But from now on, a marriage agreement will be irrelevant for us. On the way here, I was thinking that I want to hold a ceremony to sever those relations."

He took off his wedding ring and put it on the table. "Natsuki, your turn."

I hurriedly took off my ring and put it next to my husband's.

"Hold on," I said and took the tin box out of my bag. I took out the wire ring from when Yuu and I had held our marriage ceremony as children and put it down alongside them. "This one too."

"Natsuki, you still have it after all this time!" Yuu said in surprise. "My mother found my ring and threw it away. Wow, that really takes me back."

"Let the three of us now vow to divorce each other. We'll give our blessing to our end and to our new beginnings."

At my husband's urging, Yuu and I got up and stood around the table. He took our hands in his, so we hurriedly did the same, forming a circle around the wedding rings.

In a solemn voice, my husband said, "Yuu Sasamoto, do you swear that from this day forward you shall not be wedded to Natsuki and shall live as a completely separate entity from her, for better or for worse, for richer or for poorer, and in sickness and in health, and that you shall not love, cherish, or worship, nor stand by her, and shall live life for life's sake as long as you shall live?"

"Er . . . I do."

"Natsuki Miyazawa, do you also swear that you shall live as a completely separate entity from Yuu and shall live life for life's sake as long as you shall live?"

"I do."

My husband nodded solemnly and turned to Yuu. "Okay, now will you officiate our divorce for us?"

Still looking bewildered, Yuu did as my husband said and started reciting the lines to us.

"Um, Tomoya Miyazawa, do you swear that from this day forward you shall not be wedded to Natsuki and that you shall live as a completely separate entity from her, um . . . for better or for worse, for richer or for poorer, in sickness and in health, and that you shall not love, cherish, or worship, nor stand by her, and shall live life for life's sake as long as you shall live?"

"I do."

"Natsuki, do you also swear?"

"I do."

"Okay," my husband said. "The ties between us have now been cut. We are no longer family. Each of us is now just living our own life." He held his hand out to Yuu, who shook it, still looking disorientated. "Well then, we'll take responsibility for disposing of these rings. Thank you for everything. See you."

My husband and I went outside together.

"Legally we may still be married," he told me. "But we've now transcended that sort of relationship."

"Yeah." I nodded. He was still my husband, but more than that he was a Popinpobopian. This was something I could trust far more than marriage.

We had just started walking, hoping to find a main road where taxis would be passing, when we heard the door open behind us.

"Uh . . . are you leaving just like that?" Yuu asked, coming out onto the street.

"Yes, that's the idea," my husband answered cheerfully.

"Should I give you a lift? I mean . . . should I . . . um . . . why . . ." He seemed confused.

"Is something wrong?" my husband asked him curiously.

"I don't know. I've been given my freedom, but I'm not any good at being free. I'm used to following orders, but there aren't any signposts anymore. Now, or rather for some time now, I've accepted that." He seemed to make up his mind and raised his head to look at us. "I've changed my mind. I want to go with you. That's the only way I can think to make use of my freedom."

My husband beamed. "I'm delighted. Your freedom has turned out to be in the same place as ours! What kind of miracle is that?" he said, taking Yuu's hands in his.

Yuu still looked bewildered, but he said, "You've both got the Factory after you, haven't you? Best not tell Uncle Teruyoshi that you're going to Akishina. I'll call him later and tell him we all decided to go to Tokyo together. I haven't got much luggage, so please hold on," he said, urging us to get in his car and wait for him.

I still didn't understand what had prompted Yuu to come with us to Akishina, but I was glad we three creatures would be living together again.

My husband and I got into the back seat of Yuu's car.

"Oh, the moon!" my husband said.

Without my noticing, evening had been drawing in and the light-blue sky was beginning to change color. Outside the car window, the streets were taking on the glow of night. Light was blanketing the surface of the planet. Earthlings were moving busily around the surface of this glowing orb.

By the time we arrived in Akishina, the sky was thick with stars.

The house had only been empty a short while, but it already had the look of an abandoned nest. Inside, the air was stagnant and smelled of mold, and the worn pillars and tatami looked more dilapidated than ever. On the floor in the hall there was some excrement from a nonhuman animal.

Yuu seemed tired from driving. He barely said a word as we went around opening all the windows to let in some fresh air, warmed ourselves in the kotatsu, and ate some defrosted oyaki dumplings.

"The kotatsu won't be enough. I'll go get the electric heater."

My husband was breezy and cheerful.

"What shall we do from now on?" he asked.

"That's something we'll have to decide. After all, we're receptacles now," my husband said, his cheeks full of oyaki.

Yuu and I were speechless.

"Receptacles?"

"Well, we are, aren't we? We don't have a mother planet. We don't know Planet Popinpobopia at all, and we can't get back there. So, we're empty receptacles." My husband casually wiped a piece of eggplant off his lip as if wondering what our problem was. "So, from now on we'll live as receptacles. Or rather, continuing to live as receptacles is probably what it means to be Popinpobopian. Don't you reckon, Yuu?"

Bewildered at suddenly having the conversation directed at him, Yuu glanced nervously at me. "Um . . . I suppose so."

"Definitely!"

My husband seemed so sure of himself that I somehow felt what he was saying must be true and nodded cautiously. "You're probably right. After all, we're aliens, but we don't know anything about our mother planet. Other aliens are probably doing the same."

"Yes, they are," my husband said, as though he knew lots of aliens.

Yuu was still a little anxious. "But what are we going to do from now on? We might very much be Popinpobopians now, but to stay alive we need to rely on Earthling knowledge. And if we keep doing that we might become Earthlings, mightn't we?"

"We'll have to think about it. Staying alive is about coming up with ideas. Living on the ideas that we come up with." My husband frowned and sniffed.

"Ideas? Really?"

"Yes. Not imitating the Earthlings but coming up with our own ideas for living. That's how we can live on a planet that isn't our own."

Taken aback, I looked at Yuu. We had survived so far. Yuu looked deep in thought.

"First, we'll look for food. It's like we just crash-landed on this planet. We have to take a new look at the world from that perspective. We must see everything with the alien eye. This mysterious round food is really tasty. This object made of wood is warm. But let's think harder. What can we, as receptacles, do on this planet?"

"Right. But it's really cold on this planet. This thing that Earthlings call bedding seems to be just right for sleeping, doesn't it? Is it okay if I try it out over there?"

"Of course!"

Yuu took some bedding out of the closet, threw it in a heap on the floor, crawled into it, and fell asleep. He had always been so meticulous about making his bed, but now he'd simply crawled into a pile of bedding as if into a nest and was already in a deep sleep.

"He somehow looks as though he's about to be reborn," I murmured, staring at the mountain of bedding he'd made. It looked like the pupa of some strange creature.

* * *

From the next day, our way of life changed completely.

Yuu was the first to say we should train every day to avoid becoming Earthlings. We would train as Popinpobopians using the same techniques we'd drawn on during our training to become Earthlings.

There was no need to be bound to the concept of day and night, but we decided to go out on the prowl together once while the sky was light and again at an appropriate time after it got dark. To begin with, we could still sense that it was around seven in the morning, say, or three in the middle of the night, but gradually we lost any notion of time other than it being light or dark.

The feeling of being a Popinpobopian existed within us receptacles. It had just been dormant. Rather than gaining a new sensibility, it felt as though we were recovering one we'd always had.

Funnily enough, with training we progressed rapidly. All three of us saw everything from a more rational stance through our alien eyes than we had through Earthling eyes. Any time one of us creatures discovered something through alien eyes, the other two applauded it. We judged what we saw not in terms of knowledge or culture but in terms of whether or not it was rational.

I felt myself progressing faster than I ever had before. I wondered why people in the Factory didn't undertake this kind of training.

Survival was our main criterion for deciding what was rational. Getting food for that day was more important than anything else.

At first, Yuu would go out alone when it was light to steal vegetables from the garden of the neighboring house.

"I did feel bad about it, but then I thought that it was more rational to steal than use the little money we have left," he said.

We both strongly agreed with this.

"But if you get caught, it wouldn't be rational. We'll all be discovered."

"True. We have to be careful."

We decided to use money only for fuel and lighting expenses. We also decided to refrain from using heating and lighting as much as possible. Electricity for the kotatsu and heater was necessary to survive, but we hardly used it for anything else. It was easy to keep the lights off at night and live in the dark. We often used gas for cooking, but sometimes instead we made a bonfire in the garden, when we were sure we wouldn't be seen.

Procuring food without money was hard. It was more tiring than we'd imagined to hunt animals, and we felt it wasn't very rational. According to Earthling knowledge, animals that were relatively easy to catch such as rats tended to be unhygienic, but in many cases you could eat them after cooking. A lot of plants were unsafe to eat, and we had to take care when picking them.

We developed rapidly. The world looked completely different from a purely rational viewpoint. We combined the Earthling knowledge from books in the attic with the internet searches I made when I went with my phone to the other side of the red bridge.

"I wonder why the Earthlings don't seem to want to develop like us," I said.

"They can't let go of the knowledge they've accumulated, even though it's nothing more than data," Yuu answered.

We followed the needs of our bodies. The biggest issue was always appetite. For excretion, we gratefully used the device created by the Earthlings. For sleep, we simply crawled into the pile of bedding whenever we felt like it. It was warmer than laying it out the way the Earthlings did, especially as we could make use of each other's body heat when we were in there together.

The house was our lair. Inside it we often went naked, having decided that it was pointless to worry about cleanliness, changing our clothes, and doing laundry when we spent most of our time either in the bedding nest or kotatsu, occasionally crawling on all fours, or making food that spattered juice everywhere.

Even though there were two males and one female all naked, we felt a sense of security rather than unease. Neither my husband nor Yuu seemed to take any particular interest in me as a female. But that didn't mean we didn't feel any sexual urges. We often raised the topic of breeding and sexual desire.

"Given that we have both male and female, in theory we could breed, couldn't we?" Yuu murmured as all three of us sat in cold bathwater, using each other's body heat to warm ourselves to save on heating.

My husband nodded. "As far as managing sexual desire goes, we can do that alone without any need for a male and female to copulate. That would be more rational, don't you think?"

We always used to talk like this on nights when it had been easy to steal, after we had come back to our lair, washed off the mud, and were ready to sleep.

"The difference is whether we want to procreate or whether it's enough just to satisfy our sexual desires, isn't it?" Yuu said warily during one of our conversations. He was always awkward on this topic.

"If we had a child, we would be able to observe what effect our pure lives as Popinpobopians would have on this new receptacle. That would give useful data," I chimed in.

"As an experiment? I suppose that's rational," Yuu said, nodding.

"But Natsuki's the only female, so it would be a burden on her. Could we perhaps find another Popinpobopian female and persuade her to come here?" my husband suggested.

Yuu shook his head. "Let's give up the idea. It would be using the womb as a tool. And that would mean that our testes and womb would not be our own, exactly like in the Factory."

"Yes, I feel the same way about it," my husband agreed.

I was relieved they felt that way.

"Well then, we two males prioritize sating our sexual urges over procreation. What shall we do with our sperm? Just throw it away?"

"Let's think of some use for it. What about as food?"

Yuu tilted his head questioningly, and my husband shrugged.

"It must be nutritious, but I don't see any data about humans using sperm in cooking. There might be some value in trying it, but if we mix it with other foodstuff and it turns out not to taste good, it'll mean throwing all of it away, won't it?"

"I'll look up the nutritional value."

The two of them were chatting away together so casually it didn't sound even remotely like a sexual substance. To avoid being left behind in the conversation, I chimed in again.

"So we won't procreate? Is it okay for Popinpobopians to die out with just the three of us?"

Yuu rubbed his arm where goosebumps had broken out in the cold water. "Yes, I'm okay with that. It's already enough if aliens crash-landing on this planet can just survive for their natural life span. What's more, our alienness is contagious, so it's entirely possible that a Popinpobopian awakened on Earth might come from elsewhere. We're proving right now that you can become an alien through training."

"That's true. Training, not mating, is our method of multiplying. How wonderful it would be if we could take our lives forward into the future infecting people with Popinpobotitis!

Yes, let's go forth and multiply!" my husband cried, raising his fist in the air.

"Through training we awaken a new part of the human brain, a part never used until now. That's how Popinpobopians will evolve, and the data will surely be beneficial for Earthlings too."

"Well then, how should we satisfy the sexual desire in these receptacles?" I asked.

My husband and Yuu looked at each other and chuckled.

"No need to worry about that. Whenever necessary, just follow the natural course and satisfy it alone. That's the best way. It's clean and doesn't hurt anyone."

My husband agreed eagerly. "It's okay to use Earthling knowledge, but we're more likely to find the appropriate method by listening to our bodies. But we shouldn't force it. When a useless sexual desire arises, we just satisfy it, that's all. Just the same as defecating. If we didn't have the desire to defecate, there wouldn't be any need to go to the toilet."

"And what about love?" I asked.

Yuu looked puzzled. "That's completely irrational. I didn't think it was even worth discussing."

My husband looked at me quizzically. "Love is a drug made in the brain to enable humans to mate. It's simply an anesthetic. In other words, it's an illusion made to prettify the painful mating act, to reduce the suffering and disgust of the sexual act. We might be able to use this anesthetic if we're ever in pain. But for now I don't think it's necessary."

"I see," I said and got out of the bath. "I'm ready to get out. Catching a cold would be irrational."

"That's true. If it gets any colder, unheated baths will be impossible. We'll die!"

Laughing, we dried our bodies with towels and, still naked, ran to the kitchen where the food we'd picked that day was ready and waiting. Outside was tinged with the color of outer space. All too soon we were in Dark Time.

Light Time was just beginning, a pale, inky hue still left in the sky, when the Akishina house phone rang.

We had decided not to answer. Yuu said that it was more rational that way. The more it looked as though the house was empty, the easier it would be to steal as the neighbors wouldn't be on their guard against us.

We lay there in bed, still naked, waiting for it to stop ringing.

It rang insistently, at least three times, and by the time it stopped we were wide awake.

"How about we cut the telephone line? That way it won't make any noise, and the house will appear even more abandoned," my husband proposed.

"Yes, good idea!" we agreed.

It was only when I went to pick some wild herbs that I realized my sister had left a large number of voice mails on my smartphone. The moment I crossed the red bridge and reached the point where we could get reception, notifications started pinging on the phone in my pocket. I hastily took it out and put it on silent mode.

I looked at the screen and saw they were all messages and emails from my sister. She had probably been the one calling the house landline too.

Traitor! read one. I didn't quite understand what she meant by this, so I listened to a voice mail.

Come back home right now! I'll never forgive you if you break up my family too!

They all said pretty much the same thing. I had absolutely no idea what she was so angry about. If she was being this persistent it probably wouldn't be long before she turned up here in Akishina, so when I got back I talked to Yuu about it.

"I don't know the details, but maybe someone has informed Kise's husband about a private matter of hers?"

"What?" I exclaimed, shocked suddenly at hearing my sister's name. "Has she done something?"

Yuu looked taken aback. "Didn't you know? All the relatives were gossiping about how she was sleeping around a lot at work, and her husband was running a background check on her.

"Really?"

"He was apparently checking up on her right back to childhood. His parents even contacted Uncle Teruyoshi at one point."

"I wonder why they didn't contact us as well?"

"It's possible they're investigating you, too, Natsuki. But making a fuss over sleeping around is irrational, isn't it? If the idea of mating is to get your genes into the next generation, it should be laudable."

Yuu had once been so proper, but now he saw the world from a Popinpobopian perspective and simply couldn't understand why my sister and her husband and his family were making such a fuss.

"Do you want to procreate, Yuu?"

Yuu tilted his head questioningly. "I guess. It's probably rational for a living creature to do so. If we carry on like this, Popinpobopians will become extinct. But I'm not all that interested in it."

"Oh."

My husband probably felt the same way. Our nakedness around the house was innocent, as if we had returned to the time before Adam and Eve ate the apple.

Later on, the messages from my sister were still bothering me, so I again crossed the red bridge alone to check my phone. There was one new message.

You gave me away, didn't you? Even though I kept quiet about you. I know everything! And I'll never forgive you. I'll get my revenge on you for breaking up my family.

Her hatred was palpable, but given I hadn't known anything about her affairs until today, she was off the mark. Still, it looked as though things were going to turn nasty. I smashed my phone to pieces on the road and threw it into the river.

I must be in love. This irrational thought occurred to me as the three of us lay naked in bed.

I was finding it hard to sleep and had barely nodded off when I woke up again. Gazing at the light of the moon through the window, I wondered about the ache I was feeling in this receptacle.

My sense of smell and hearing had been sharp these last few days, and I had the feeling that my body was awakening. My cells, which had been tense all this time, were now relaxing as I spent time naked with my two fellow Popinpobopians.

I had thought my sexual urge was broken and that I would never in my life experience it again. But now that my flesh was in a state of utter relaxation, for the first time a sexual urge was forming. This was a phenomenon that only happened when the three of us were all together.

Long ago, before Mr. Igasaki, I sometimes felt a sweet sexual sensation stirring within me as I lay enveloped in blankets or surrounded by soft toys. This was similar, though I felt reassured by the contact with Yuu and my husband's flesh in a way I had never experienced before.

But it was so irrational! I should train harder. Yet the sensation that my own flesh had been restored was a blessing for me.

Maybe this would be an anesthetic I thought, so I should keep it in reserve. It might come in useful should I experience intense pain for any reason.

Hoping with all my heart that I would never have to use it, I went to sleep fantasizing that the three of us were putting our lips together in a kiss. A pleasant, cozy sensation tickled at the backs of my kneecaps.

* * *

"The road farther along the mountain has been closed," Yuu informed us first thing the next morning.

"Really? It snowed yesterday I guess," I answered, unconcerned.

"That amount of snow is nothing for this area, quite normal. No, there must have been a landslide. There have been quite a few lately."

My husband had been extremely excited when the first snow fell in Akishina. I had only ever been to my grandmother's house in summer, so the snowy landscape felt fresh and beautiful to me too.

According to Yuu, real snow in this area was a completely different affair. It could be life-threatening, so it would be better if it didn't snow so much over winter. My husband, a city boy who hadn't seen snow in the countryside before, sat for ages gazing at the garden, now and then making comments like "It's so beautiful!" and "Does snow count as a food?"

"There isn't much sign of Earthlings in the village, is there?" I said to Yuu when I came back inside.

We had all gone out in search of food. I had gone to the river to catch insects, and Yuu and my husband had been out gathering plants.

Yuu nodded. "The snow yesterday was more like sleet, which makes the area prone to landslides. Most of the Earthlings probably went down into town since they realized the road might get blocked."

"I see. That makes it easier to steal food, doesn't it?"

"How convenient!" my husband said happily.

Yuu and I looked at each other and laughed.

That day we stole a lot of food and had a feast. There really were hardly any Earthlings left in the village. Faint light came from the odd house occupied by a sole, elderly resident, but all those households with someone capable of driving had gone down to the valley. Most people here didn't bother locking their doors, so we were able to brazenly go in and steal lots of food—not only rice and vegetables but apples and oranges too.

"Somehow it feels like the Last Supper, don't you think?"

"Christ's Last Supper was simple fare with bread and wine," Yuu said with a shrug.

"That's not what I mean. Just tonight somehow conjures that image."

"No doubt the Earthlings will send us to the gallows for stealing so much from them," my husband said, stuffing his face with the first fruit he'd tasted in a long time.

"If all the Earthlings disappear, Popinpobopians will reign over this village!"

"Yeah! It'd be great to live with a different culture and customs. We'd have to take care not to become like the Factory, of course."

We chatted about silly things as we drank the sake we'd stolen. I still couldn't taste anything, but I ate a lot that day.

Enjoying the warmth of the sake that Yuu heated for us, we carried on drinking until late.

It was the first drink I'd had for ages and in my drunken state I sang nonsense songs while my husband clapped along and Yuu watched us, laughing.

It was a perfect night. I went to sleep dreaming of how wonderful it would be to wake up and find the village full of Popinpobopians. In my dream, my sister and parents and my mother- and father-in-law had all become Popinpobopians, and the party went on forever. The breathing and vibrations of my husband and Yuu as they slept crossed the boundary between dream and reality. Their warmth crept up close to me as I laughed in my dream.

I awoke to a sharp blow on my head. Groggy with pain and sleepiness, I opened my eyes a fraction and saw in the darkness a faint line of light pointing upward and forming a circle on the ceiling.

Reflexively I rolled over the floor away from the barely visible beam. There was a loud thud from the place where until moments ago I had been fast asleep. The room shook.

"Are you human?" I shouted instantly.

Peering into the dark I could make out a large creature brandishing something in its hand. Its body recoiled, startled by the sound of my voice.

I jumped up and ran to the cabinet once used by my grandfather. My eyes were gradually adjusting to the dark, and my body was moving faster than my mind. My survival instinct had kicked in, and all my head was telling me was that I had to bring down the intruder.

There was no sign of Yuu or my husband. Maybe they'd already been killed.

The black figure didn't seem to be familiar with the house and appeared confused, bumping into walls as it moved around. From the sound of its breathing, I was sure it was an Earthling.

If it was an Earthling and not a bear, I stood a chance. Before I knew it I'd grabbed a trophy my grandfather had won for calligraphy and was waving it around. Instinct drove my body faster than my brain could issue instructions. Aiming for where I thought the face would be, I brought the heavy trophy down on it with all my strength.

I hit my mark. It was more of a crunch than a snap, and I felt a sticky liquid cling to my fingertips.

Got it! I thought and quickly raised the trophy and brought it down two or three more times on the same place.

"Aaah! Gyaaaahhh!"

I'd known that it was an Earthling, but until I heard it scream it had never occurred to me that it might be female. But I couldn't take anything for granted. I straddled the weakened crouching lump, bashing it mercilessly with the trophy until I was certain of victory.

"Stop! Stop!"

I had no idea how much I had to weaken it to be a hundred percent sure of my own survival, but as long as it had a voice there was a chance of it counterattacking, so I kept hitting it, aiming for the spot where I thought its face was.

I continued my attack until my opponent went limp. Then, just to be sure, I wound the electric cord from the kotatsu tightly around its neck. Still uneasy, I grabbed the cord from the hot water pot and bound its wrists. Cautiously keeping the trophy at the ready, I turned on the light.

A small woman was lying in a much bigger pool of blood than I'd expected. In the dark she'd appeared so large I'd thought she might be a bear, but now in the light I could see she was a rather frail-looking elderly woman. Lying next to her was a golf club, presumably the weapon she'd first hit me with. I quickly grabbed it and added it to my own armory. I felt a little easier.

I wondered whether my husband and Yuu were safe. There might still be other enemies. Making as little sound as possible, I went to check the bedding mound.

My husband was lying beside the pile. I rushed over and shook him. He groaned and opened his eyes.

"Tomoya, are you okay?" I asked, relieved.

"Natsuki? What happened? All I remember is that we'd been drinking and then went to sleep, and the next thing I knew something whacked my head."

"There are Earthlings in the house trying to kill us. I caught one of them, but there are probably more. What about Yuu?"

"I don't know."

I rummaged around in the bedding, but Yuu wasn't there. "Maybe he got away. I hope so."

I went to the kitchen to get a knife, just in case. Just then I heard a loud noise outside. Clutching the knife in one hand and the golf club in the other, I ran outside. It was still Dark Time, but amid the gloom I saw a pool of light.

Looking closer, I saw it was a car with its lights on. Inside, Yuu and a large man were grappling.

"Yuu!" I called.

"Yuu!" my husband echoed.

At the sound of our voices, the man turned and paled. "You! You're the one who murdered our Takaki!"

He lunged at me, but Yuu sent him flying with a kick from behind. My husband pounced on him as he lay there dazed. I passed him the golf club.

"Thanks."

He took it clumsily, apparently still groggy, and hit the man with it.

Now that the man was weakened, I stabbed him in the eyes with the knife. Once his movements were completely dulled, I kept stabbing him in the neck and heart, aiming for where he would bleed most.

"He came by car in the middle of the night to kill us I suppose."

The man was slumped, still, no longer breathing or screaming, but I couldn't be sure he was dead. I continued stabbing him almost as if I was preparing him for cooking. At my side, my husband kept beating him with the golf club.

"You two, you can stop now," Yuu said calmly. "He must be dead, and at this rate he'll end up as mincemeat."

"What happened?"

"I was sleeping when suddenly a hand was clamped over my mouth and I was dragged out to the car. He was looking for someone, apparently."

"Me, probably," I said.

Both Yuu and my husband raised their heads and looked at me.

"Takaki was the name of a teacher of mine, Mr. Igasaki."

"So who was he?"

"I killed him, back when I was in elementary school. These are his parents."

I'd thought the late-middle-aged woman looked familiar. These were the people who had always been handing out leaflets outside the station. How had they found out that I was their son's killer? I had no idea, but I knew very well why they had come after me so ferociously. I had killed a member of their family. Killing a person was irrational. Even if you killed just one, decades later their family would still be bent on revenge.

My husband and Yuu were staring at me. The man's body briefly shuddered. Instantly I stabbed him again with the knife. I still felt that he could come back to life at any moment, so I carried on stabbing him. This time neither Yuu nor my husband restrained me. They just watched as blood spurted everywhere.

* * *

Now that we had forgotten about time, we had no way of knowing what stage Dark Time was at or whether Light Time would come soon.

"I'll go check on what's happening in the village," Yuu said. He put on some clothes, got into his car, and started the engine.

My husband and I wound packing tape around the two Earthlings, then rolled them to the entrance hall of the house, still unsure whether they were completely dead.

"We're in trouble. There's been another landslide down by the bridge," Yuu told us when he returned about an hour later. "There must be a few Earthlings left in the village, but this is the only house this side of the bridge that isn't empty. We're the only ones left behind."

"Did these Earthlings cause the landslide deliberately?"

Yuu shook his head. "I don't know. The first landslide at least was natural. They often happen around that spot. I think these Earthlings probably took advantage of there being not many other Earthlings around on the mountain to come and kill us. I don't know whether it's just coincidence that the mountain pass has been blocked by a landslide or whether they caused it to stop us from getting away. But they could only have caused it by using some kind of explosive, and that's not something you can get hold of easily."

We found some pieces of evidence in the Earthlings' bags: a recording of the conversation with my sister in the karaoke room, an old, partially burned scythe, a pair of bloodstained socks. It must have been my sister who had given them these things. She had known everything all along. The evidence I'd hidden in the furnace had disappeared because she'd retrieved it and kept it all this time.

I didn't know why my sister had decided to take revenge on me now. I suppose her "family" must have broken up, and emotionally it was rational to blame someone else.

"I'm sorry. It's my fault. I killed their son, so I must be the one they came after." I was being dragged back into the Earthlings' world. It was as if I was being woken from a dream.

My husband frowned at my apology. "No, these Earthlings are out of order. Why should they come to kill you just because you killed their child? I could understand it more if they came to demand you provide them with a descendant to the human race. After all, the Factory exists as an organization for Earthlings to procreate. But even though they surely count you as an Earthling, they deliberately come here to further reduce their numbers by their own hand. It's completely irrational."

Yuu peered closely into my face. "Why did you kill the teacher?"

"Because I thought that I would be killed if I didn't."

Yuu gave a little smile. "Survive, whatever it takes, right?"

"What's that?" my husband asked curiously.

"Our motto when we were kids," Yuu said.

"That's great. Apart from anything, it's a really pure motto. And it's absolutely correct too," my husband said.

"Well then, how are we going to survive from now on? The road is blocked, and we're trapped here alone. We always kept the lights off, so it's very likely the villagers thought this house was unoccupied. But we have to do everything in our power to survive, whatever it takes."

Yuu and I nodded emphatically.

Snow was beginning to fall. Countless irregular lumps of shredded ice fell around us, coloring the ground white.

We laid the corpses of the two Earthlings out in the entrance hall and went to sit in the living room.

"I guess all we can do is wait," Yuu said.

My husband and I nodded.

"I wish we hadn't cut the telephone line."

"No, it was the most rational thing to do at the time. We have water, and there's still some of the food we stole left. The Earthlings from the Factory are bound to come after us, so I think the landslide will be discovered relatively quickly."

"We'd been thinking of how to shake off of our pursuers if they came, but now we're waiting for them, are we?"

My husband sighed. "I want you two to survive, Yuu and Natsuki, but if it means being taken back to the Factory, then I'd rather stay here myself. Being taken back there I might as well be dead."

"Tomoya, don't say that. Earthlings have a habit of saving their own kind, so let's use them to get out of here. Then we can escape somewhere else."

I rubbed my husband's back.

* * *

When Light Time and Dark Time had repeated some three times, we realized that we'd been overoptimistic.

Our stash of stolen food was practically gone. There were two other houses cut off by the landslide, and we had eaten all of their food.

"Shall we freeze the Earthling meat while it's still fresh?" Yuu proposed suddenly.

"Are Earthlings edible?"

"They're animals, aren't they? They're relatively clean animals, too, so I don't suppose there's much risk of disease. I think perhaps we should preserve them as emergency food while we still have the option, before they rot."

"I guess so." I nodded, but in the back of my mind was the thought that if we did this, we would lose any chance of ever being accepted into the Earthling fold again.

"I did once kill a chicken I was given by one of the local people here. I've never butchered large livestock, but I think it's probably necessary to drain the blood from them. I don't have anything better to do with my time, so I guess I could do that."

Yuu made this proposal with the detachment of a true Popinpobopian. He was clearly easily influenced by his environment. He had been the best at fitting in and pretending to be an Earthling, and he was also the best at training to be a Popinpobopian.

"I'll help, Yuu. It looks like it'll be heavy work." My husband stood up.

"Thanks," Yuu said. "Let's start with the small one."

They went to get the body still lying by the front door where we'd left it.

I cowered alone in the room, unmoving. There was probably still some human left in me.

By the time I plucked up the courage to open the kitchen door, Light Time had returned, and the pair had just started work on the larger of the Earthlings.

"I'll help too."

Yuu turned to look at me. "Natsuki, don't force yourself. It's heavy work, after all."

"It's true, it takes quite a bit of strength. We're probably not doing it right," my husband said.

"It's okay, I'll help," I told them. "I want to." I held out a knife I'd found in the attic. "I think this will work better than a kitchen knife."

"Thanks. To tell the truth, the first one didn't go too well. Scraping the flesh off made it all pulpy like mincemeat." Yuu smiled.

"Can I try?"

"Go ahead. We're basically following the method for butchering pigs, but I'm not sure if it'll work since the body's constructed completely differently."

"What should I do first?"

"Cut off the head and drain as much blood off as possible."

I stuck the knife into the man's throat.

"It's hard, isn't it?" my husband said. "We used a saw."

I switched tools and put all my strength into the task. The bones were really hard, but with some help from the others I finally managed to cut off the head. It landed on the floor with a thud.

"Right, let's raise the body up and drain out as much blood as we can."

Together we picked up the body and held it upside down over the sink. Now that they were on the second one, Yuu seemed to be getting used to things. He widened the opening so that the blood flowed into the sink.

"That looks tasty," I murmured. Seeing the exposed red flesh, my stomach started rumbling.

"It does, doesn't it? All the food's gone, so should we have some of this tonight?"

"Yes, let's!"

Once we started cutting up the Earthling, it was nothing more than a large piece of meat. Following Yuu's instructions, we split open the torso, removed the innards, and washed the corpse. It smelled worse than I'd expected, and I grimaced. We washed the meat as well as we could, then carved it away from the large bones.

My husband and Yuu started getting the utensils ready so we could start cooking as soon as the preparations were finished.

"We have seasonings, so shall we boil it in miso? It stinks a bit, so would probably be best with a strong flavoring."

"We've still got some daikon leaves. I bet it would taste good fried up with those."

"Yeah, maybe. The freezer is already full of the woman, so the rational thing to do would be to eat whatever won't fit in. Let's try different ways of eating it."

"We'll have a feast tonight!" my husband cried happily.

We prepared three Man dishes: Miso Soup with Man, Daikon Leaf and Man Stir-Fry, and Man Simmered in Sweetened Soy Sauce.

"It's been ages since we last sat down to a spread like this, hasn't it?" my husband said in delight, and Yuu concurred happily.

I was hungry, too, and could hardly wait to tuck into the man. It was the first time I'd felt such a fierce appetite since my mouth had been broken.

"Bon appétit!"

I took a sip of the Miso Soup with Man and got quite a shock. "I can taste it!"

"What do you mean? Of course you can! It's food, after all," Yuu said, amused, but I felt a surge of excitement at sensing taste on my tongue after such a long time.

I'd thought my mouth would never recover as long as I lived, but now it was my own again. The meaty soup filled my entire mouth with the strong flavor mixed in with the smell and slowly saturated each part of my body. Ecstatically,

I munched on the Earthling. I felt as though I was eating for the first time in twenty-three years.

The Earthling was really delicious. No doubt it tasted even better since I was hungry and also because I was so fond of the two creatures I was sharing it with.

"I wish there was still a bit of sake left," my husband said.

We both agreed with him and raised our glasses of well water for a toast. Then we carried on eating the man.

For the first time in so long I felt satiated. Dark Time stretched and grew into an eternity as we felt the comforting presence of the creatures of the mountain all around us.

Our bellies full, we took some quilts to the kotatsu, wrapped ourselves in them, and dozed. Since today was a special day, Yuu brought a candle from the altar room and lit it for us. It was the first time in ages that we'd been enveloped in a glow of light during the Dark Time, and it felt somehow like a ceremony.

The three of us creatures wrapped in pure white quilts, dimly discernable in the candlelight, resembled cocoons. Maybe this is what the silkworm room had looked like, I mused sleepily.

According to Uncle Teruyoshi, after the silkworms had swelled up and taken over the whole house, the Earthlings would remove the tatami mats to expose the floorboards in the living room and the two large tatami rooms to let them become the domain of the silkworms. The Earthlings, meanwhile, slept in the corners, listening to the sound of silkworms munching noisily on mulberry leaves everywhere in the house.

I wondered what the Earthlings dreamed of whilst sleeping among countless pure white cocoons. As I dozed, I imagined what it must have looked like with the white insects wriggling around all over the room.

"I've got a request," Yuu said abruptly as we lay in our quilts, our sighs of satisfaction beginning to blend into snores.

"What's that?"

"If things carry on like this and the Earthlings don't come for us, I want you to eat me."

My husband and I jumped in surprise, our drowsiness immediately dispelled, and the plate of Earthling stir-fry by my husband's hand spilled onto the floor.

"It's far better than all three of us dying, and you already know how to butcher and cook me. Rather than us going extinct, it's much more rational for you two to eat me and survive."

"But in that case we could equally eat Tomoya or me, couldn't we?"

"Yes, but I want to be the one who decides how to use my own body. I was never any good at handling freedom, but now for the first time I feel that if I am really free then that's what I want to do."

My husband frantically leaned forward and grabbed the edge of Yuu's quilt. "Yuu, there's got to be a more rational way. Like, how about we each cut off an arm or a leg and eat them all together? That way the three of us can survive."

Yuu shook his head. "If we do that to these receptacles, we'll probably die right away. It'd be okay if there was a surgeon among us, but none of us have the skill or the equipment. It's safer to eat one of us at a time."

I thought a moment, then said, "Well then, after Yuu, Tomoya should eat me. Of the three of us, I think he should be the one to survive. He's the biggest and strongest and will last the longest once the food completely runs out."

"Why are you both talking like this?" my husband shouted, shaking his head petulantly. "We made a pledge, didn't we? We swore to live as completely separate entities from each other, for better or for worse, for richer or for poorer, in sickness and in health, that we would not love, cherish, or worship, nor stand by each other, and would live life for ourselves as long as we lived, right?"

Yuu and I looked at each other. Even Yuu seemed to understand that my husband was evidently not going to give way on this point.

He gently slid the spilled Earthling stir-fry back onto my husband's plate and said, "You're right, we did make the pledge. Well, how about this? How about we all taste a little bit of each other and then decide to eat each other in the order of how good we taste? If something is unpalatable, we probably wouldn't be able to finish eating it. And there's no need to cut off a finger or whatever in order to taste each other. We can just take a nibble."

"Yes, that's fair! I think that's very rational," I agreed.

My husband appeared satisfied with this suggestion. "Okay. Yes, that's best. If I taste the best, be sure to eat me all up, okay?"

First of all, my husband and I took a bite each out of Yuu, me from his shoulder and my husband from his arm, testing the flavor on our tongues. He tasted slightly salty.

My husband apparently thought the same. After a few more bites, he said, "There's a good hint of salt, so we could probably eat you without adding any seasonings. If we decide on eating you first, I promise to cherish you as food."

"Me next," I said.

Nervously my husband bit into me. "Ugh, bitter!" he said. "We might all be Popinpobopians, but we taste completely different."

Yuu took a bite out of his own arm, then licked my knee wonderingly. "Mmm, there's a slightly metallic taste. Maybe the taste of your blood is coming through." He removed his tongue from my knee and bit my husband's index finger.

"What do I taste like?" he asked.

"A bit sweet."

"Really?"

We started eagerly taking bites out of each other, commenting on the flavor.

"I'm so hungry! Even though we've just eaten an Earthling."

My husband sighed. "I can't tell which of us tastes best."

"At this rate, we're going to eat each other all up."

We each gnawed on bits of thigh and back and heel and jaw. I felt a raging hunger. Yuu and my husband were both delicious.

Eventually we were not satisfied by the surface alone and started in on each other's innards with our teeth and tongues.

While having his eyelid chewed, my husband muttered, "Since coming here, I sometimes wonder whether there really are any true Earthlings at all. Maybe we're all Popinpobopians. We were Popinpobopians from the start, and Earthling brainwashing worked for everyone except us three. Earthlings are just an illusion created by Popinpobopians to enable us to live on another planet."

Crunching on my husband's elbow, Yuu agreed. "You're probably right," he said quietly. "That means nobody will come to rescue us. They've probably all woken up from the dream, and now with the alien eye they'll have realized that it wouldn't be rational to come and rescue us."

I was too busy eating the two of them to join in the conversation. They would be so delicious with some steamed white rice I thought. Now that I'd recovered my taste buds, I was savoring the various flavors: sweet, bitter, sour, salty.

"Oh, my ear!" I suddenly exclaimed.

"What about it? Is it tasty?"

I didn't answer but sank my teeth into the thigh before my eyes.

My right ear had been broken all this time, but now there was a sound like wind exploding and the buzzing completely disappeared. Suddenly the sounds of the world began streaming in.

The first thing that entered my liberated ear was the sound of our meal. It made my eardrum shake and quiver. The sound rushed into me.

"Survive, whatever it takes," I whispered in a small voice. That voice, too, fell inside my right ear and slowly made my eardrum vibrate.

That day, my body became completely my own.

Outside the window, it was beginning to snow. The shining white powder reflected the candlelight inside as it fluttered down from outer space. I thought of the scales that silkworms have. I imagined what it must have looked like when countless silk moths took to the air, shedding scales as they flew around the room.

The snow falling from the pitch-black sky was turning the ground white. The snow obliterated the presence of the creatures outside, and the only sound that remained was that of our uninterrupted meal in the flickering candlelight of the room.

A little while later, it was Light Time. The scent of Earthling reached me as I dozed, and I opened my eye a crack.

My head still sunk into the warm pillow woven from Earthling hair. I ran my eyes casually over the tatami and saw a finger lying there. I had been sucking on the bone, and it had rolled out of my mouth as I slept.

I reached out for it, still covered in saliva, and put it back in my mouth. It still tasted faintly of meat, and I sucked on it slowly, savoring the flavor.

The windows and doors should all have been closed tight against the cold of the fresh snowfall, but a breeze came in from somewhere and ruffled my hair. With it came a whiff of Earthling, sweet like wild boar meat soaked in milk but blended with an animal stench.

"Popinpobopia?"

I slowly raised myself up and turned my face toward where the stench was coming from. Through the paper shoji I saw a pale glow, as though reflected off the snow.

Piyyut lay sprawled out by my ankle. I picked him up and hugged him to me. Piyyut looked different now and was woven from a mass of black, gray, and white Earthling hair. He snuggled up to me.

As I cuddled Piyyut in my arms, the backs of my legs picked up the vibration of the floor creaking. I leaned forward and reached out a hand to a thigh lying on the floor. I grabbed it and shook it hard.

"Tomoya!" I whispered.

My thin, bony husband responded to my shaking. Instantly he wrapped his arms protectively around his swollen belly and slowly opened his eyes.

He had fallen asleep while eating some arm soup we'd made during Dark Time. I gently put the bowl on the TV stand, careful not to spill any of the precious food, and called to the other creature lying next to my husband.

"Yuu."

Yuu's belly was even more swollen than my husband's. His thin skin was stretched taut, and the bones and swollen belly within it stood out clearly.

"Popinpobopia," Yuu responded in our language, rubbing his eyes.

Just then, the creaking of the floor grew louder, and with it came the sound and vibration of footsteps as the smell of Earthling abruptly grew stronger. Yuu and my husband raised themselves up and we huddled our bodies together. Yuu and my husband held their arms protectively over their swollen bellies, and I clutched Piyyut to my chest.

Aiiiiiieeeeeeeeeeeee!

I wondered what that sound was for a moment, before realizing it was an Earthling's scream. My sister appeared through the door, took one look at the three of us, and screamed again.

Aiiiiiiiieeeeeeeeeeeeeeeeeeeeeee!

Mom was just behind my sister, and their shrill screams resonated through the room.

There were more footsteps as other Earthlings came running, alerted by the loud cries. A number of other Earthlings clad in orange suits clustered behind Mom. Judging from their attire, I thought they were probably Earthlings who performed the role known as a rescue party.

"Earthlings," I muttered.

The rescue party Earthlings took one glance at us huddled together and grunted, holding their hands over their mouths.

"Are you . . . human?" an Earthling male finally managed to squeeze out as he stared at us.

The three of us looked at each other.

"Popinpobopia?"

"Popinpobopia."

Gently rubbing his swollen belly protectively with his right hand, Yuu started speaking to him in fluent Earthling language.

"We are from Planet Popinpobopia. You are, too, aren't you?"

Liquid spurted from the man's nose and mouth as he stood there, although I wasn't sure if it was saliva from the shock or if he was bringing up gastric juice.

"What are those . . . bellies?" another Earthling male next to him asked, his voice hoarse.

"The three of us are pregnant," my husband said, holding his belly up with both hands for them to see.

The Earthlings started shaking and took some steps back away from us, their faces pale.

"Don't worry," Yuu said. "This form of yourselves is also dormant within you, even if it isn't evident now. It can infect you at any time." He smiled at them reassuringly. "Tomorrow we will multiply. The day after we will multiply more."

The Earthlings didn't seem to be listening to Yuu's careful explanation. One at the back was violently throwing up.

"Shall we go outside? Our future is awaiting us," Yuu said to us, and we nodded.

Gently entwining our arms and legs together, we three Popinpobopians rose up. From the outside world, the glow of Light Time with its reflection from the snow softly flowed into our spaceship.

Holding hands, shoulder to shoulder, and engulfed in light, we slowly stepped out onto the Earthlings' planet. As if in concert with us, the cries of the Earthlings rang out to the far corners of the planet, setting the forests trembling.

Keep in touch with
Granta Books:

Visit granta.com to discover more.

GRANTA

THE INTERNATIONAL BESTSELLER

CONVENIENCE STORE WOMAN

Sayaka Murata

Translated by Ginny Tapley Takemori

'Irresistibly quirky' *Guardian*, 'Books of the Year'

'Hilarious . . . I couldn't put it down' Elif Batuman

'Exhilaratingly weird and funny' Sally Rooney

'As intoxicating as a sake mojito' *Vogue*

Keiko doesn't fit in.

She's 36 years old, she's never had a boyfriend and she's been working in the same convenience store for eighteen years.

Her parents wish she'd get a better job. Her friends wonder why she won't get married.

But Keiko knows what makes her happy, and she's not going to let anyone take her away from her convenience store . . .

'Quirky, memorable . . . it could only be Japanese' *The Times*

'This novel made me laugh. Absurd, comical, cute . . . audacious, and precise' Hiromi Kawakami, author of *Strange Weather in Tokyo*

'A deadpan gem . . . This is a true original' *Daily Mail*

'Dreamy' *New Yorker*